THE PLAY OF

Buddy's Song

NIGEL HINTON

Questions and activities by Lawrence Till

Series Editor: Lawrence Till

Heinemann Educational Publishers
Halley Court, Jordan Hill, Oxford OX2 8EJ
a division of Reed Educational & Professional Publishing Ltd
MELBOURNE   AUCKLAND
FLORENCE   PRAGUE   MADRID   ATHENS
SINGAPORE   TOKYO   SAO PAULO
CHICAGO   PORTSMOUTH (NH)   MEXICO
IBADAN   GABORONE   JOHANNESBURG
KAMPALA   NAIROBI

First published in 1994
First published in the *Heinemann Plays* series 1994
2000 99 98 97
10 9 8 7 6 5 4 3

A catalogue record for this book is available from the British Library on request.
ISBN 0 435 23306 8

Cover design by Keith Pointing

Original design by Jeffery White Creative Associates; adpated by Jim Turner

Typeset by CentraCet Limited, Cambridge

Printed by Clays Ltd, St Ives plc

CONTENTS

Acknowledgements

The Songs

'Taking the Blame', 'A Girl like Peggy Sue', 'I'm Young', 'It's gonna be Tough', 'Brain Train', 'Feel so Alive', 'Ordinary Girl' by Nigel Hinton and John Wesley Harding. © 1990. Lyrics reproduced by permission of Trinifold Music Ltd and Plangent Visions Music Ltd.

'I'm a Man not a Boy' by Nigel Hinton, John Wesley Harding and Chesney Hawkes. © 1990. Lyrics reproduced by permission of Trinifold Music Ltd and Plangent Visions Music Ltd.

'Secrets of the Heart', 'Torn in Half' by Nigel Hinton and Chesney Hawkes. © Lyrics reproduced by permission of Trinifold Music Ltd.

'This is Me' by Nigel Hinton, Thom Hardwell and Alan Shacklock. © 1990 Lyrics reproduced by permission of Trinifold Music Ltd.

'Love's Nothing Serious' by Nigel Hinton and Greg Palmer. © 1993. Lyrics reproduced by permission of the authors.

'Keep on Searching', 'Buddy's Song' by Nigel Hinton and Steve Morley. © 1989 Lyrics reproduced by permission of the authors.

'The One and Only' by Nik Kershaw. © 1990 Warner Chappell Music Ltd, London. Lyrics reproduced by permission of International Music Publications Ltd.

INTRODUCTION

Nigel Hinton's novels *Buddy* and *Buddy's Song* have long been two of the most popular novels in schools. Here, Nigel tells us how the play version of *Buddy's Song* developed from the original story:

This musical play was written twelve years after the character Buddy Clark first started to come to life in my head. Twelve years in which the character grew and developed and his story was told in different ways.

Buddy began life as a story about an eight-year-old boy called Stuart who mishears something his parents say and starts to believe that his cousin is a spy. I got halfway through then abandoned it – it wasn't doing what I wanted it to do.

I knew what I wanted the book to explore: the feeling I had when I was growing up, a feeling shared by many young people, that I didn't quite understand what was going on in the adult world. There seemed to be so much withheld information, so many half hints and mysteries. These adults were in control of my life and I assumed that they did what they did for good, rational reasons so I couldn't understand why things seemed to be in such a mess. Of course, since becoming an adult, I realise it's not true that things operate by good, rational rules – we often just muddle through in a fog of confused and conflicting emotions.

Eventually I hit on a better story for exploring this idea. A bright fourteen-year-old boy believes that his mother has left home because he stole some money from her purse. The truth is that she's left because she can no longer cope with her husband, Terry, an ageing Teddy Boy. Terry – crazy about music, into clothes, feckless, and on the fringes of crime – is more of a teenager than his son. And as soon as I realised that Terry was a Teddy Boy I knew that he would have named his son after his favourite singer,

Buddy Holly, so Stuart became Buddy. Now I had the main elements of the plot: a boy, mistakenly filled with guilt about his mother's departure, schemes to bring her home while trying to keep his father from falling further into crime. I was ready to write the book.

Four years after the book was published, BBC Schools TV made a film serial of *Buddy*. Everybody involved was very enthusiastic about the project and during the filming they kept jokingly asking when I was going to write *Buddy 2*. I had no intention of writing a sequel but one day on the set I saw a guitar against a cupboard in Buddy's bedroom. I asked the set designer why it was there and he said, 'Don't you think Terry is the sort of dad who would buy an old guitar for his son and that Buddy would have played it a bit and then shoved it away to gather dust?'

It was a brilliant bit of set design and I couldn't stop thinking about it. Yes, I thought, and when Buddy's plans to reunite his family fail and his dad gets caught by the police, he would learn to play that guitar in order to make a tape of Buddy Holly songs for his dad in prison. It would be his way of saying sorry. The plot for *Buddy's Song* started there.

While writing the book I knew that I wanted the songs to be very important – Terry had always used other people's music to express his feelings, putting on a record to say 'I love you' or 'Sorry'. Buddy, like his dad, finds it hard to say things directly, but being more intelligent and creative, he would write his own songs to say what he felt. I started jotting down lyrics and three of them were put in the book.

When I wrote the script for the film version of the story, as well as changing the story a bit for the big screen, I added more songs. Although the soundtrack album was a big success and we even had a number one hit single, there was never time in a ninety minute film for more than a brief snatch of each of the songs. I felt, vaguely, that the songs still hadn't taken their rightful place at the centre of the story – as Buddy's way of expressing his feelings about being half in and half out of that confusing adult world.

So when I was approached to write a stage version I jumped at the chance. I had always liked stage musicals and I thought that perhaps I could finally use the songs properly. The finished product isn't exactly a musical, more a play with a lot of songs, but it has a lot in common with that form.

For a start, I wanted the songs to flow naturally from the action. So, for example, Buddy and Julius talking about girls leads directly to 'A Girl like Peggy Sue'. Or when Buddy tells his parents to stop treating him like a kid, we immediately see him singing, 'I'm a Man not a Boy', a song he's been inspired to write because of his row with them. In the same way, every song is relevant to what has just happened in the play.

This allows the songs to comment on the action and give a greater insight into how Buddy feels. For example, the song, 'Love's Nothing Serious', tells us some of the hurt and disappointment Buddy feels over losing Elaine – and it tells us more briefly because Buddy can say things more directly in a song than he would ever say to someone else.

And again, Buddy would never be able to tell his parents face to face how he feels about their break-up, so he pours all his anger and sorrow and pain into 'Torn in Half'. At the same time this link between the songs and the action shows how writers of all kinds – novelists, playwrights, songwriters and poets, or even someone writing a story for school homework – often use their experience as a jumping-off point for their writing.

In the film of *Buddy's Song*, all the songs were sung by Buddy but for the stage version I wanted to have other people sing too, as they do in musicals. Three of the songs that Buddy had sung in the film immediately seemed suitable.

'The One and Only' had been sung over the closing credits of the film but the more I thought about it, the more I realised that it was a perfect song for Terry – the eternally optimistic individual emerging from prison still declaring that there's nobody he'd rather be.

In the film, 'Secrets of the Heart' had been sung by Buddy but it hadn't really fitted in to the story. As soon as I gave it to Carol and Terry though, it became a perfect way of showing the confusion and sadness of their break-up. When they sing from opposite sides of the stage about 'even standing side by side, we still live so apart', the song fills in so much about their relationship that I didn't have time to put into the play.

The way that a song can so quickly sketch something that it would take ages to do in dialogue is best shown in 'Feel so Alive'. In the film it was used as background music to show Buddy's romance with Elaine, but in the play I decided to have all three couples – Buddy and Elaine, Terry and Dawn, and Carol and Adrian – sing it as they all wander arm in arm round the night streets of the town. It was a wonderful shorthand way for showing them all having the same magical experience of falling in love.

When I finished writing the playscript I hoped that I had taken the best bits from the book and the film and put them into an entirely new shape with the music right at the heart of it. I was then very lucky to have the play put on by a company that brought the very best out of it. I was there for nearly half of the rehearsals and it was a delight to watch the director, the technicians and the actors bring the play to life. The cast was wonderful. Nearly all of them played more than one part, doubling up as waiters, policemen, etc., and we were very lucky also to have some great pupils from local schools who helped to create atmosphere in crowd scenes.

For me though, the biggest thrill was watching the work of the actors who played Buddy and the band. All of them had only a limited experience of singing and playing instruments but I saw them become, through fantastic hard work (and a lot of fun), a real band. They looked like a band, talked like a band, and played like a band. They even started thinking of themselves as a real band and played a number of gigs in pubs. Needless to say they added all sorts of improvised lines to their parts and I've included some of them in this finished script.

The actual shape of the play, with rapid switches of time and location, was partly determined by the fact that I was writing for a specific theatre – The New Victoria Theatre in North Staffordshire – which is a purpose-built theatre in the round. Having the audience all round the stage, and having a large number of possible exits and entrances for the actors, encouraged me to make the action as free-flowing as possible.

Sets and props were kept to a minimum – a table and chairs became a pub, an armchair and a table became the Clark home, a bed was a prison cell – lighting and sound effects were used to create mood for each scene. Only one part of the acting area was constant: the band area, since it would have been impossible to keep moving the amps and drum kit. So the band area served as rehearsal space, youth club, night club, recording studio, etc., with different lighting effects to distinguish them, and some movement of the mikes to ensure that no one part of the audience saw the back of the band all the time. I think the play would work just as well on a normal stage but even there, it might be useful to have an additional acting area, on the floor of the auditorium perhaps, to make sure that the action kept flowing smoothly without too many slow scene changes.

Nigel Hinton

Nigel Hinton's biography

Nigel Hinton was born and brought up in London. He worked in advertising before becoming a teacher and an actor. He has written three books for young children, four for teenagers and one for adults. His books have been translated into many languages. He has also written for TV, including the highly successful 5-part serial of *Buddy*.

He is married, and lives in Kent. His main interests are rock music, especially the work of Bob Dylan, swimming and films.

*This playscript is dedicated to
the wonderful team who were involved in
the first production of the play at
The New Victoria Theatre,
North Staffordshire.*

List of Characters

The first production of *Buddy's Song* took place at the New Victoria Theatre, North Staffordshire from 30 June to 24 July 1993 with the following cast:

Buddy	Bob Golding
Terry	Neil Phillips
Carol	Sarah Mortimer
Des King	Peter Cleall
Julius	Daniel Beales
Jason	Gary Turner
Glenn	Nicholas Haverson
Adrian	Clive Moore
Dawn	Karen Chatwin
Elaine	Pandora Ormsby-Gore

Director	Rob Swain
Designer	Zoe Bacharach
Musical Director	Greg Palmer
Choreographer	Sue Harris
Lighting Designer	Alex Forsyth
Sound Designer	James Earls-Davis

Buddy's Song

Nigel Hinton

ACT ONE

Scene One

Teddy Boy Convention. A large banner hung above the stage declares: 10th Rockers' Hop. The song 'See You Later Alligator' by Bill Haley is playing while a crowd of Teds and their girls dance.

As the song approaches the end we become aware of Terry Clark who is standing on one of the stairways. He is bopping and singing along with wild abandon, much to the embarrassment of his fifteen-year-old son, Buddy, who tries to look as if he isn't with him. The song ends.

Terry Yeah! Rock 'n' Roll! Rock 'n' Roll!

Buddy Dad.

Terry What?

Buddy Cut it out. Everyone's looking.

Terry Yeah – I'm a right little star.

Terry waves at a woman then at Dougie, one of the Teds dancing.

Wotcher, darling – all right? Hey Dougie!

Dougie Terry! How are you doing?

Buddy Dad.

Terry Don't be such a square. Here, you ought to meet Dougie – he could give you some guitar lessons.

Buddy I don't want to learn that kind of stuff.

Terry It's the greatest music in the world – better than all that modern rubbish. I don't get you – I buy you a guitar for your birthday and you don't even bother to learn it.

Buddy I am learning it but I want to play my own songs.

There's a call from behind them. It's Des King, Terry's old friend. King is the man behind all kinds of unlawful operations and Terry has often done little 'jobs' for him. King is outrageously dressed in a gold lamé suit although he's not quiffed and side-burned like the real Teds.

Des   Terry!

Terry   Des! Woah, look at you.

Des   The business. Hello Buddy.

Buddy merely acknowledges King with a nod.

How you doing, Tel – haven't seen you for a while.

Terry   Yeah, great.

Des   Here, you lost some weight, ain't you? Where's Carol?

Terry   She's . . . not here.

Des   Oh?

Terry   No, didn't fancy it . . . Oh, may as well tell you, Des – we've split up.

Des   You're joking. When?

Terry   Four months ago.

Des   I don't believe it. What – another bloke?

Terry   No, nothing like that. She said she . . . needed space.

Des   Space? What she think she is – a bloody astronaut? Cor, Terry, that's a killer. I mean she was always independent, was Carol, but you've been married for . . . what?

Terry   Twenty years.

Des   Stone me. Buddy living with you, is he?

Terry   Yeah. We get along great, don't we?

Buddy makes a sort of agreeing shrug. Des King's portable phone rings.

Des   Now what? Hello . . . Hello, love . . . What? . . . Now calm down. When? No, you shouldn't have told them that. No, I know you didn't, dear. All right, look I'll sort it. 'Bye. And a big one from me, too.

He puts the phone back in his pocket.

Terry Trouble?

Des Cops been round my house. She's only gone and told them I'm here. Listen – you got your motor here?

Terry Yeah.

Des Do us a favour – I've got a small case I don't want found. Can I dump it in yours till they've gone?

Terry Course – anything to help a mate.

Des Ta – I'll go and get it.

Des goes off. Terry knows Buddy is furious but he tries to change the subject.

Terry Here, how about some music?

He speaks to Buddy

What you looking at me like that for?

Buddy You promised. You promised you wouldn't get mixed up with him again.

Terry I'm not getting mixed up.

Buddy Course you are. It's stolen stuff in his case.

Terry Maybe – but I didn't steal it, did I? I told you I've stopped all that. Do I ever lie to you?

Buddy Yeah – all the time.

Terry OK – sometimes, you cheeky bugger. But not now. You heard him. I can't let an old friend down, can I?

Buddy Mum's right – you'd jump off a bridge if Des King told you to.

Terry Yeah, well, your mum doesn't know very much about loyalty does she?

Buddy walks away. Terry goes after him.

Buddy. Buddy. I'm sorry – I take it back about your mum. I didn't mean it. But I just can't let a mate down.

Des comes back carrying a briefcase and calls to Terry.

Des Where's your motor then, Tel?

Terry looks at Buddy in an appeal to understand, then shrugs and goes up the steps towards Des. We hear the first verse of 'I Fought the Law'. Buddy checks his watch. The song continues quietly under the dialogue as Buddy spots Julius who's carrying a bucket and sponge.

Buddy   Hey, Julius – what you doing here?

Julius   Making money, buying an electric bass and changing my sex life.

Buddy   What you on about?

Julius   You see this bucket? This bucket is sex.

Buddy   Eh?

Julius   Step One: all these guys are nuts about their American cars outside. I wash the cars. The guys all pass me mega-money. Step Two: the money helps towards buying a bass guitar. Step Three: we form a band. Step Four: we become superstars. Step Five: every young girl in the universe lusts for my perfect body. Step Six: I give in to their wild desires. Then I pass them on to you.

Buddy   Oh thanks.

Julius   I've even figured where we can start playing – the shopping precinct. There are always buskers down there.

Buddy   Listen, I gotta go – I'm meeting someone.

Julius   Oh-ho, a date.

Buddy   My mum.

Julius   Your mum?

Buddy   It's a surprise. See you later.

Julius goes. Buddy spots a uniformed policeman and an Inspector in plain clothes. Buddy looks at them as they go past then he starts in the direction his dad went to warn him but Carol calls to him.

Carol   Buddy.

Buddy   Mum!

Carol Hello, love.

Buddy You look great.

Carol Hardly dressed for this lot, am I? Honestly Buddy, I don't know if this is a good idea.

Buddy Of course it is. Oh, don't let me down. You promised.

Carol Don't look at me like that. Buddy, lots of marriages break up.

Buddy So what? It doesn't make it easier.

Carol Surely anything's easier than listening to us two row all the time.

Buddy It won't be like that. Dad's changed. He's got a job now.

Carol I've seen it all before. He gets a job then one day he bumps into Des King or one of the others and they tell him about this little plan they've got. I know him. He's weak.

Buddy Don't say that.

Carol It's the truth. I don't want to sit around any more, scared that the cops are gonna knock on the door any minute. And anyway, I've changed. I've got this job; I'm meeting new people. I don't feel the same.

Buddy You still love him, though. You do, don't you?

Carol God help me. Yes, I still love him.

Buddy Please. Just come and say hello.

Carol shrugs an agreement. Lights out on Carol and Buddy. Lights on Terry who is sitting with a Teddy Boy who has a guitar singing the Buddy Holly song 'Crying, Waiting, Hoping'. Halfway through, Terry sees Carol and Buddy as they come in. He stops singing for a moment then finishes the song making the words his message to her. At the end he comes over to them.

Terry Hello Carol. You look fabulous.

Carol Thanks. You look . . . the same as ever.

Terry You know me – I never change.

Carol Buddy said you had.

Buddy   I told Mum about your new job.

Terry   Oh yeah – I got a new job.

Carol   Buddy told me.

Terry   Down at the bookies.

Carol   Yeah?

Terry   Yeah.

Buddy   Why don't you go and sit down – I'll get you some drinks.

Buddy goes off and Carol and Terry sit.

Terry   Buying us drinks? Did he set all this up?

Carol   He wants us to get together again.

Terry   Yeah, well, that's not up to me is it? I'm sorry, I didn't mean it like that. Listen, I've been over it all a million times and at the end of it all I know is that I miss you like crazy. Are you still living at whatsername's?

Carol   Joyce. Yes.

Terry   I bet that's a bundle of laughs. Has she made you burn your bra yet?

Carol   Don't start. She's been fantastic to me. And it's not about burning bras – it's about . . . having bigger ambitions.

Terry   Yeah, well. You look fabulous. So what about this new job of yours?

Carol   Oh, I was so lucky to get it. It's in advertising. And I just went there as a secretary really. But I started working for this top Account Executive called Adrian Mandell. And now I'm his personal assistant.

Terry   Good money?

Carol   Quite good, yeah. But the best thing is he's given me so much responsibility. He's sent me on a computer course and he wants me to learn Italian because we do a lot of business there.

At this moment Buddy comes back with the drinks.

Buddy   Here you are. Dad, can I have the keys to the car? I think I left some money in there. Thanks. Everything all right?

Terry   Yeah. Now get lost, you little schemer.

Buddy goes.

Carol   He's getting so tall.

Terry   Yeah. It's weird, sometimes you look at him and he's all grown up then the next minute he's like a little kid. He misses you.

Carol   I know. I thought it would be better like this. But he says he'd rather have us together even if we row.

Terry   Us row? What's he on about? We could try stopping. I mean we don't have to row, do we? We could try being nice to each other.

The lights go down on them and up on Buddy who is on another level. He's got the case Des gave to Terry.

Buddy   Julius!

Julius comes out, car cloth in hand.

Julius   What?

Buddy   Seen that Jag outside? I want to get into the boot. I'm not nicking anything – I just want to put this in. Can you open it?

Julius   See these fingers? Houdini would've killed for them.

The lights go out. We hear Buddy Holly's song 'True Love Ways' during which the lights come up on Terry and Carol.

Terry   Here, it's 'True Love Ways'. Remember this? The first time I saw you – down the Salt Box Café. You were with that fat friend of yours – erm . . .?

Carol   Paulette.

Terry   Paulette! God, she was horrible. You were a right looker, though. Still are. I was dead scared to ask you.

Carol   Scared! You were dead cocky. You walked straight over, grabbed my hand and said, ''Ere you, want to dance with the best-looking bloke in the room?'

Terry   Yeah, always modest. Well, do you want to dance
            with the best-looking bloke in the room? Come on –
            for old times.

            *Carol allows herself to be pulled to her feet and they
            begin to dance. Terry joins in the singing of 'True
            Love Ways', making his statement to Carol. During the
            instrumental break they stop dancing as Terry talks.*

            What about giving it another go?

Carol   Terry, things have changed.

Terry   Nothing's changed. Nothing. I still love you. Come on,
            let's try – for Buddy.

            *He pulls her close again and sings the song again. As
            the song finishes, Buddy, who has been watching
            from the shadows, applauds as they come off the
            dance floor.*

Buddy   You dance really well.

Terry   Yeah, well, we're made for each other, aren't we? Do
            you want another drink?

Carol   I'll get them.

Terry   Oh no.

Carol   Oh yes – I'm a liberated wage-earner now. No
            arguments.

            *As she's talking, Terry sees Des King walk past with
            the Inspector and Policeman. So he doesn't argue.*

Terry   OK, then.

            Carol goes off.

            Give me the keys. I'm just gonna move the car.

Buddy   You don't need to. I put that case back in the Jag.

Terry   You did what? My prints are all over that case. You
            stupid little . . . Stay here and look after your mum.

Buddy   Dad.

Terry   Stay here.

            Terry runs off leaving Buddy. Carol comes back in.

Carol   What an idiot. I threaten to pay and then forget my
            bag. Where's your dad?

Buddy   Oh . . . just gone to check something in the car.

Carol   What do you want to drink? Coke? What's the matter?

Buddy   Nothing. A coke, yeah.

Carol goes off. Buddy waits until she's gone then heads off in the direction Terry took. The lights come up on another level where Terry has got the briefcase. He comes face to face with the Inspector who is accompanying Des King. Terry stops, turns, and tries to make a break for it down a stairway. He's stopped in his tracks by the other Policeman who is mounting the stairs. He turns and goes back. The Inspector holds his hand out for the case. Terry gives it to him.

Inspector   Well, Des, I'd say we've found what we're looking for, wouldn't you?

Des   I've never seen that case before in my life.

Inspector   Oh, Des – you're not going to let Sonny Boy here take the rap for you. Oh, Des, that's nasty. What about you Sonny Boy – are you going to tell us whose case this is? You're a fool. OK, we'd better go down to the station. There's some more questions I want to ask you.

Terry and Des are being led away when Buddy appears.

Buddy   Dad!

Terry hesitates a moment at the sound of the call then he continues to move away. The lights go out. In the darkness a Judge pronounces sentence on Terry from off stage or as voice over.

Judge   Terence Colin Clark, you have pleaded guilty to receiving stolen goods. Although the charges of theft against you have been dismissed for lack of evidence, you have a long record of similar crimes so I have no hesitation in sentencing you to twelve months in prison.

In the darkness, a cell door clangs shut.

Scene Two

The Clark's living room. Buddy has his guitar. He's in the process of making up 'Taking the Blame'. He strums gently and experiments with what he's written of verse two. Buddy sings.

Buddy   The night sky's so lonely
The stars look so sad
I promise tomorrow
I won't let you down
Every time that I hurt you.

He goes over the last line again, searching for the next line.

Every time that I hurt you

He stops then tries:

Something good in me dies

He adds the new line to the page he's writing the song on.

Something . . . good . . . in me . . . dies.

He starts the song again. The door opens and Carol comes in. She's been to the prison. She takes off her coat and slumps in a chair.

Buddy   Hi. How's Dad?

Carol   As usual. Talk, talk, talk a hundred miles an hour. Jokes about this, jokes about that. One big act.

Buddy   Did he say anything?

Carol   He asked if you were OK.

Buddy   I'm going to do a tape for him. A load of Buddy Holly songs and maybe a couple I've written. What do you think?

Carol   I think he'd be more pleased if you went to see him. I mean it, Buddy – it's four months now. If you could see his face every time I turn up without you.

Buddy can't stand this. He gets up and heads for the door.

Running away doesn't change anything.

Buddy stops.

Buddy   Mum, how can I go and see him after what I did?

Carol   Is that what this is about? You didn't do anything. He's the one who got himself in this mess and he's the one who's got to live with it. Not us.

There's a ring at the door. Buddy goes and answers it. He comes back with Des King.

Des   Hello Carol.

Carol   What do you want?

Des   It's private.

Carol   Say it in front of him or not at all.

Des   Carol, what can I tell you? Things went wrong. God knows what he was doing with that bloody case. If he'd left it where it was . . . Anyway, Terry's bad luck. Could've happened to anyone.

Carol   Not to you, Des. Somehow, you're not the type that ever gets caught, are you?

Des   Look, they'd got him. There was no point in both of us going down, was there? Anyway, however you look at it, I owe it to Terry to make sure you're looked after.

Des brings out an envelope stuffed with £50 notes. He holds it out.

Carol   We don't want your blood money.

Des   Come on, Carol . . .

Carol   We don't want it.

Des knows it's no use. He pockets the money and heads for the door. He stops.

Des   Listen, if there's ever anything you need . . .

Carol   You'll be the last to know.

*Des goes. Carol and Buddy look at each other. The
lights go out.*

Scene Three

*Terry's cell. Terry is lying on his bed. He gets up,
takes a cassette tape out of its box and puts it on his
small cassette player. He switches it on. The lights
stay on him.*

*Buddy's room. As Terry switches the cassette player
on we see Buddy making the tape that Terry is
listening to.*

Buddy It's been all Buddy Holly songs so far but I've got a bit
of space left so I'm going to put on one that I wrote
myself. Don't laugh!

*He strums the guitar a couple of times then starts
singing.*

SONG: ***Taking the Blame***

The road's dark and empty
I'm walking alone
I'm trying to reach you
Cos I let you down
Got so much inside me
But what can I say
There's a high wall between us
That won't go away.

Chorus

I've been crying all night
And calling your name
Not making excuses
You know how I'm feeling
You're feeling the same
Not making excuses
I'm taking the blame.

Terry now joins in from his cell and they sing the rest of the song together.

The night sky's so lonely
The stars look so sad
I promise tomorrow
I won't let you down
Every time that I hurt you
Something good in me dies
No use pretending
The truth's in my eyes.

Chorus

How could it happen
That our lines got so crossed
You're paying the price
I'm counting the cost.

Chorus

The lights go down on Buddy. Terry switches off the cassette player and sings the chorus to himself. As he ends there's the sound of a cell door opening.

Warder   Come on, Clark. You've got visitors.

The lights go out on Terry and come up on the Prison Visiting Area. Carol and Buddy sit down at a table. Buddy is nervous. Carol checks her make-up. Terry comes in.

Terry   Hello love. Wotcher mate, you made it this time, then?

Buddy   Yeah. Dad, I'm sorry about . . .

Terry   No sorries. No sorries about nothing, right? You look great, Carol.

Carol   How are things?

Terry   OK, yeah. Here, what about this one, then?

Carol   What?

Terry   The tape! His tape! You must've heard it – it's fantastic.

Buddy   Did you really like it?

Terry   It's the business. I've played it to loads of blokes in here and they all reckon you're gonna be a star. Just think, I could be your manager. You and me together, eh?

Carol   Don't start filling his head with ideas like that. I want him to concentrate on his school work.

Terry   School work! Waste of time.

Carol   How would you know – you never did any.

Terry   Elvis, Buddy Holly, Little Richard – they didn't get to the top because of school work, did they?

Carol   What's that got to do with it? I bet most of the blokes in this place didn't do any school work either and look where it got them.

Terry   Oh, like me I suppose.

Carol   I didn't mean that. It's just . . . exams are important. And he's done really well with his GCSE's and I want him to go on to do his 'A' Levels.

Terry   A's, ECG's. It's all rubbish.

Carol   No, it's not rubbish. It's hard work. And it's having a sense of achievement. I know – because I've just passed my computer exams. Thanks for asking.

Terry   Yeah, well I don't know why two bloody geniuses like you waste your time visiting a dummy like me.

Terry gets up, sending his chair tumbling. He goes a few paces then stops, comes back, picks up the chair and sits.

Come on, don't let's row. You're right – I was a lazy little bugger at school and look where it got me. Not much longer though. I've had some good news.

Carol   What? Oh come on Terry, what?

Terry   I went in front of the parole board, Thursday. And if I'm a good boy and don't murder the Governor they're gonna let me out in two months.

Carol   Oh, Terry, that's wonderful.

Terry   Yeah. Here, they don't do champagne at the canteen but we could always celebrate with a cup of tea.

Carol   I'll go and get them.

Carol goes.

Terry   So. School's OK, then?

Buddy   Yeah, it's OK.

Terry   A right brainbox. What about your mum? She OK?

Buddy   Yeah, fine.

Terry   Goes out a bit, does she?

Buddy   Sometimes. She's usually working though.

Terry   Oh yeah – at the office.

Buddy   Yeah.

Terry   Late?

Buddy   Yeah – there's always some rush job on.

Terry   Buddy . . . if . . . if she started seeing someone else, you'd tell me, wouldn't you?

Buddy   She wouldn't.

Terry   Couldn't blame her. I mean, I made a right bloody mess up, didn't I?

Buddy   She wouldn't though.

Terry   Maybe. It's just that you get a lot of time to think about it in here. Anyway, keep your eye open, won't you.

Carol comes back with three cups of tea.

Carol   Oh, I've forgotten the sugar.

Buddy   I'll go.

Carol sits down and passes the cups as Buddy exits.

Terry   Some of the blokes in here won't drink this stuff – reckon it's spiked with tranquillisers to keep 'em quiet. Lowers the sex drive.

Carol was about to drink. She looks dubiously at the cup.

Carol   It's not, is it?

Terry roars with laughter.

Terry Don't worry – I'll still have enough lead in my pencil to keep you happy when I get out of here.

This joke doesn't make Carol laugh and just before the lights go out on them Terry stops laughing and they look at each other.

Scene Four

Julius's room. Julius preens in front of a mirror. He's got a bass guitar and he plucks it rhythmically if not, as yet, all that skilfully to the basic beat. He looks at himself and chants.

Julius Sex, sex, sex, sex, sex, sex . . .
Girls, girls, girls, girls, girls . . .
Sex, sex, sex I want it
Girls, girls, girls, I want them . . .

Buddy has come in during this. He's carrying his guitar. Julius is startled to see him as Buddy laughs.

Buddy You're obsessed with sex.

Julius And you're not, I suppose.

Buddy No. I'm just healthily interested.

Julius Oh yeah, twenty-four hours a day healthily interested. Anyway, I'm not obsexed . . . er obsessed. I just want to know two things: why are girls so wonderful? and how do I get one? It ought to be easy like in a song. You know like 'Peggy Sue, I love you' and bang you're in bed with her.

He pounds his bass to the following:

Peggy Sue, I love you
Let's go to bed and have a . . . cup of tea

Buddy strums his guitar and composes the following lines:

Buddy I wish I knew

A girl like Peggy Sue
I wish I knew, now, Peggy Sue.

Hey – it's not bad.

He keeps strumming and sings it again. Julius joins in.

Julius Yeah, it's good. Why don't you work on it and we could sing it in the precinct on Saturday.

Buddy Listen, Jules, you're not serious about this precinct thing.

Julius Course, I am. We've got to get used to performing in front of an audience.

Buddy Julius, shoppers are not an audience.

Julius You kidding? Think of all those beautiful girls hanging around the precinct on a Saturday lusting for a bit of action. Loads of big names started off busking, you know. I won't be able to use my guitar, of course, but I've solved that – I'm gonna use a tea-chest bass. Just think – our first real gig. Roll on Saturday.

The lights go out.

Scene Five

The Shopping Precinct. The noise of traffic and shoppers. Some people stroll around shopping. Julius comes on with a tea-chest bass, followed by a reluctant Buddy with his guitar.

Julius Here's a good place.

Buddy What about down the other end?

Julius No, there's less people down there.

Buddy Exactly. God, I hope no one from school sees us.

Julius You've just got first night nerves. You'll be fine once you start off. OK, let's do that 'Peggy Sue' one.

Buddy Jules, I've only just finished that one.

Julius   It's fresh in your mind then, isn't it. Come on. One,
          two, three, four.

          *Julius starts plucking the bass and Buddy has no
          choice but to join in. Buddy sings 'A Girl like Peggy
          Sue' with Julius joining in the choruses. People pass
          by. Some stop and stare. On the last chorus Julius gets
          really animated and, moving his foot from the outside
          rim to the centre of the chest, his foot goes through
          and the song ends lamely.*

          SONG: *A Girl Like Peggy Sue*

          I've got girls on my mind
          They're driving me crazy
          They look so pretty and so fine
          But really they're such a mystery
          Distant stars that always shine
          Try to think of cool things to say now
          But something always gets in the way now

          Chorus

          I wish I knew a girl like Peggy Sue
          I wish I knew now Peggy Sue
          I wish I knew a girl like Peggy Sue
          I wish I knew now Peggy Sue

          Is it magic that they've got
          That keeps me from sleeping
          I want to know, I want to give it a shot
          Cos you know now it ought to be easy
          Catch my breath and melt inside
          But when will I be satisfied.

          Chorus (I wish I knew, etc.)

          Everyday
          I'm a-waiting for
          True Love Ways
          Maybe Baby
          I'll find a girl
          Like Peggy Sue
          Oh Boy
          What I want to do

Is whisper Words of Love
That's how it happens in songs
Why can't it happen to me.

Chorus (I wish I knew, etc.)

Bloody thing. You'll just have to go on on your own
and I'll clap or something.

Buddy   Oh no – that's it. I should never have listened to you.
You made us look like complete idiots.

Julius   OK, I agree this was a bit of a mistake but listen I've
got this really brilliant idea.

Buddy   Oh no, I've had enough of your brilliant ideas.

*At this moment Buddy spots Carol strolling with
Adrian Mandell. Adrian points at something and they
laugh. Carol puts her hand on his arm – it's friendly
and could even be affectionate. Buddy turns away,
hoping not to be seen.*

Julius   No, listen, this is different – I've been in contact with
this band. There are only three of them, right, and
they're looking for a singer and a bass player. What
do you think? What do you think?

Buddy   Yeah, maybe.

*Julius goes over to his tea-chest bass and Buddy
seizes the moment with Carol's back to him to run off
in the other direction while Julius chatters on.*

Julius   Great. I'll get in contact with them and fix up an
audition or whatever you call it and then . . . Buddy?
Here, what about giving me a hand? Bloody hell.

Julius picks up the bass and exits after Buddy.

Scene Six

*The Clarks' House. Carol comes in from work
carrying files that she's brought home. The phone is
ringing – she picks it up.*

Carol   Hello? . . . Adrian, hi. Yes, I've got it. I thought I could do some work on it this evening. Look I can bring it back if you . . . Isn't it out of your way? No, of course not. Well, listen, why don't you stop and have something to eat? No, no problem at all. Fine. 'Bye.

Carol puts the phone down. She's pleased.

Buddy! Buddy!

Buddy comes in. He's dressed to go out and he's carrying his guitar.

Great – I want you to help me clear up.

Buddy   Mum . . .

Carol   No arguments – I want this place tidy. Look at this – socks! You've got a cupboard, you know. Upstairs. These books, too. And then I want you to grate some cheese and peel some potatoes.

Buddy   Mum, I'm going out.

Carol   Where?

Buddy   I've been telling you for the last two weeks but you just don't listen. I've got an audition with a band tonight.

Carol   You said it was the weekend.

Buddy   It's been changed.

Carol   No.

Buddy   What do you mean, no? It's an audition – I've got to go.

Carol   I've told you, I don't want your music getting in the way of your school work.

Buddy   It's not getting in the way. Look, I've done my homework – right?

Carol   I said no and I mean it. Buddy, look: I know all this music is important to you, and that's great. But there are other things that are more important. There's no point looking like that – it's true. Honestly, you act as if I'm your enemy or something. I'm not, you know. I just don't want you to waste your opportunities at school like I did.

Buddy I'm not wasting them.

  Carol I know you're not. And I'm really proud of how well you've got on – that's why I don't want you to let things slip. Anyway, my boss is coming round and I'd really like you to meet him.

Buddy Adrian Mandell? What's he coming here for?

  Carol He's picking something up and I asked him to have something to eat with us. You want to ask him about the importance of a good education – he'll tell you.

Buddy I bet he will.

  Carol Don't be so sarcastic. If you end up with a job half as good as his –

Buddy I don't want a job like his. Advertising! It's just telling lies to make people buy things they don't want. Anyway, I'm fed up with hearing about Adrian Bloody Mandell. Adrian does this, Adrian does that. You sound as if you're bloody in love with him.

Carol slaps Buddy round the face. He doesn't retaliate or move. They stare at each other for a moment.

Don't . . . don't you ever hit me again, Mum. Ever.

  Carol Buddy, I'm sorry.

Buddy I'm going to the audition and nothing's going to stop me, right? Nothing's going to stop me.

Carol turns away unable to continue the confrontation and Buddy leaves.

Scene Seven

Rehearsal Area. The Reflections – a three piece band of drums, guitar and keyboards – are being instructed in Buddy's songs by Julius. As the lights come up, Jason, the flash lead guitarist and Glenn, the drummer, are thrashing chords and drums loudly.

Mike, the much quieter keyboardist is trying to talk to Julius but the noise is too much.

Mike   Shut up! Shut up!

Jason and Glenn can't hear. Mike finally simply switches off Jason's amplifier and the guitar stops so Glenn stops, too.

Jason   Here, don't touch my amp – right?

Mike   I'm trying to work.

Jason   OK, but don't touch my amp or I'll ram your keyboards down your throat.

Mike   Don't mind him, Julius – he comes across as an animal but underneath it all he's really . . . a pig! OK, so where did we get to?

Julius   G to D7.
Nothing's gonna stop me
Nothing's gonna stop me
Nothing's gonna stop me – C – now.

Then the verse starts again in G. What do you think?

Mike   Yeah, it's pretty good. He wrote all of these?

Mike holds up handful of song sheets.

Julius   He writes about two songs every day. He's a total genius.

Jason   Here, what are you, his manager or something?

Julius   No – I just know when something's gonna work. And this is gonna work. It's got all the elements. Trust me. I tell you what, though – if you need someone to manage the band: I'm your man. Bass player and manager – I could handle that.

Glenn   Hold on. You ain't even part of the band yet.

Buddy comes in.

Buddy   Hi.

Julius   Where you been?

Buddy   Sorry – I got held up.

Julius   Buddy – this is Jason, Mike, Glenn. The Reflections.

	I've been going through some of your songs with them.
Jason	Yeah, and he's told us all about the other bands you've played with.
Buddy	The other bands?
Julius	Yes.
Buddy	Oh those. Yeah. Listen I don't know what Jules has told you but those songs . . . I've only just started writing and –
Mike	They're good. Really good.
Buddy	Yeah? You really think so?
Mike	Yeah. I like what you're saying in the lyrics.
Buddy	Yeah, well. I just write what I feel.

Jason reads.

Jason   I've got girls on my mind
                They're driving me crazy.

Buddy	Yeah, that's just about –
Julius	Sex. He's obsessed.
Mike	Taking the Blame?
Buddy	Oh yeah, that was kind of . . . That one's private.

Mike puts it down and picks up 'I'm Young'. He reads.

Mike   And this one?
                I've practised in the mirror
                Thinking big and walking tall
                So tired of the waiting
                Now I want it all.
                Nothing's gonna stop me . . .
                Is that how you feel?

Buddy	Erm . . . Yeah. I guess it is. I mean I really want to make it in music.
Glenn	Me, too. And nothing's gonna stop me either.
Mike	You got the drummer on your side. How about we play it?
Buddy	Sure. You know the chords? OK, well, the tempo

should be pretty punchy. Kind of 'Dee, dah, dah, dah, dah-dah'.

Glenn   Got it.

Buddy   OK then.

Jason   Let's go.

Buddy   A-one, a-two. A-one, two, three, four.

SONG: *I'm Young*

Goodbye to the playground
Now I'm free at last
Got a lot of living in me
And I wanna live it fast
I've heard that love's the best thing
To make your garden grow
I'm hungry for some loving
You can call me Romeo.

Chorus

I'm young, nothing's gonna stop me
I'm young, want it on the run
I'm young, nothing's gonna stop me, nothing's gonna stop me
Nothing's gonna stop me now.

I've practised in the mirror
Thinking big and walking tall
So tired of the waiting
Now I want it all
Don't care how rough the game gets
'Cos I can pay the price
I'm feeling good and lucky
So it's time to throw the dice.

Chorus (I'm young, etc.)

Dreaming but not sleeping
These dreams are for real
Fly high like an eagle
I'm sharpened up like steel
I run just like a cheetah
I burn just like the sun

I'm cool just like an iceberg
I'm a monkey just for fun.

Chorus (I'm young, etc.)

Jason Wow!

Julius Excellent! That was better than sex.

Glenn Oh yeah. How would you know?

Mike How'd it sound to you?

Buddy Yeah it was good but –

Mike But?

Buddy It needs work.

Mike Yeah, you're right it does. So when do we start working?

Julius Does that mean we're in?

Mike looks at the others who nod.

Mike Yeah, OK, you're in.

Julius Yeah! I knew it.

The lights go out.

Scene Eight

The Prison. Terry is just getting his belongings back from the Prison Guard prior to leaving.

Prison Guard Sign here.

Terry What's it like out today?

Prison Guard Cold and pouring with rain. You're gonna get wet, Clark.

Terry Great. It'll wash away the stink of this place.

Prison Guard You love it. That's why you keep coming back.

Terry Not this time. I got plans.

Prison Guard Oh yeah. I know your type. Six months and you'll be back. You'll never change.

Terry comes out of the prison to where Carol and Buddy are waiting under an umbrella. He turns back to the Prison Guard.

Terry You know what? You're a prat!

Terry runs and grabs hold of Carol, knocking the umbrella away. Carol laughs, caught up by his excitement.

Carol Terry, we'll get wet.

Terry Who cares! I'm free. And you're here. And it's the three of us again.

He pulls Buddy into the hug.

Blimey, you ain't half grown. Whoah, smell that air!

He lets go of Buddy and grabs hold of Carol.

Give us a kiss, darling.

Buddy smiles, thrilled, as Terry kisses Carol. Everything seems wonderful.

Everything's gonna be different now. And I swear on my life I'm never going back in prison.

He kisses Carol again then ruffles Buddy's hair.

Right, where's the nearest pub? And Carol's paying.

He puts his arms round Carol and Buddy and they head towards the pub. Des King comes from behind.

Des Terry!

Terry Des!

Carol Terry, no.

But Terry shakes off her restraining hand and goes over to Des.

Des Welcome back to the wicked world! Thought I'd turn up and buy you a drink. Fancy one?

Carol Terry –

Terry You kidding? I'm dying for one.

Des Come on, then.

Terry guides the reluctant Carol and they enter the pub.

Double scotches for you and me. What do you want, Carol?

Carol   Nothing.

Des   A gin, go on.

Carol   Nothing.

Des   What about you, Buddy?

Buddy   A lager.

Terry   Get him a shandy.

While Des is at the bar, Carol, Terry and Buddy sit down.

Carol   You said everything was going to be different.

Terry   It is.

Carol   You'll never change.

Terry   Don't say that. Look I meant what I said but that doesn't mean I have to forget my mates does it.

Des comes over carrying the drinks. He sets them down and drinks.

Cheers.

Des   Your health. Now then, there's a couple of things to sort out. First off, you need a job. Well, I've got one going down at my breaker's yard. Nothing fancy – just driving around picking up wrecks and bringing 'em back to the yard – but jobs ain't easy to get. Especially when your references come from Her Majesty's prisons.

Terry   I'll take it – thanks.

Des   Have a bit of a rest and you can start whenever you want. Now, second –

Des brings out an envelope stuffed with £50 notes.

Carol turned this lot down, but I'm hoping you won't be so stubborn.

Carol looks at Terry. They hold the look then Terry takes the envelope. Carol gets up.

Terry   Where are you going?

Carol   Home.

Terry   Carol –

But Carol goes.

Take no notice. You know Carol.

Des   Yeah, well, who can figure women? God bless 'em. Anyway Tel, I'm glad you took it. I can't ever thank you enough – you know that.

Terry   Nah, forget it.

Des   No, I'll never forget it. Well, I'll love you and leave you. See you at the yard – when you're good and ready.

Terry   You're on.

Des goes. Terry looks in the envelope and riffles through the notes.

Bloody hell. Tell me – honest: what would you have done?

Buddy   I'd have taken it.

Terry   Cheers. 'Ere, I tell you what, we'll go and buy you an electric guitar so you can start playing with a band.

Buddy   Dad – I've already got a band.

Terry   What, you and Julius? That's not a band. Come on, let's go.

They set off out into the streets of the town.

The one thing about being in nick I had loads of time to figure out what I'm gonna do as your manager. I've got real plans for you.

Buddy   Dad, you can't be my manager. I mean . . . I'm not even a proper singer, am I?

Terry   You gotta start thinking big. I didn't call you after Buddy Holly for nothing, did I? Look, all my life I listened to all those people who told me I was nothing. Well they're wrong. And I'm gonna prove it – with you. The two of us, together – we'll show 'em. All them teachers at school, all them people at the prison – they always said, 'We know your type, Clark'. Well, I'm not a type. There's only one of me.

The Reflections, minus Buddy, play behind the song while Terry sings.

SONG: ***The One and Only***

I am the one and only – nobody I'd rather be
I am the one and only – you can't take that away from me.
Call me, call me by my name
Don't call me by a number
You put me through it
I'll still be doing it the way I do it
And yet you try to make me forget
Who I really am
Don't tell me you know best
I'm not the same as all the rest.

Chorus (I am the one and only, etc.)

I've been a player in the crowd scene
A flicker on the big screen
My soul embraces
One more in a million faces
High hopes and aspirations
Ideas above my station
Maybe, but all this time I tried
To walk with dignity and pride.

Chorus (I am the one and only, etc.)

The music continues under the next sequence as Terry puts his arm round Buddy and leads him into a guitar shop. He talks to the shopkeeper.

Terry   I want the best guitar you've got in the shop.

Shopkeeper   Certainly, Sir.

Buddy   Dad, they cost a fortune.

Terry   Got to have the best. Here, there's this Ted band I know. They play all the big Rock 'n' Roll festivals. I reckon I can fix some gigs with them. Be a great start.

Buddy   I already sing with some –

Terry	That's the one! Beautiful. Plug it in and have a go. Now, how much you gonna knock off it if we take an amplifier as well?
Shopkeeper	I'm afraid we don't do discounts.

Terry flashes the envelope of notes.

	Except for cash, of course. Five per cent?
Terry	Ten.
Shopkeeper	I'm sorry.
Terry	Come on, Buddy, we're off.
Shopkeeper	Ten it is.
Terry	Twelve and a half. Take it or leave it.
Shopkeeper	Twelve and a half it is.

Meanwhile Buddy has plugged the guitar in.

Terry	Right then, let's hear what you can do.

He plays the chord that sends Terry into the rest of the song with The Reflections playing along behind.

SONG: ***The One and Only*** (continued)

I can't wear this uniform
Without some compromises
Because you'll find out that we come
In different shapes and sizes.
No one can be myself like I can
For this job I'm the best man
But while this may be true
You are the one and only you.

Chorus (twice) (I am the one and only, etc.)

The lights go out.

Scene Nine

The Clarks' house. Carol is working on a home computer or on files brought home from work. Terry and Buddy come in with their purchases. Classical music is playing softly from a cassette player.

Terry Da Da! Surprise!

Carol looks up then goes on with her work. Terry goes up to her, pretending to be videoing her.

And here she is, folks, the star of our show, Carol Clark!

Carol Terry, I'm working.

Terry Too busy to have your present then.

Terry holds up a necklace.

Carol What's this?

Terry What's it look like? Been shopping. Guitar for Buddy. This for you. And the camera for me. And I've had a brilliant idea – I'm gonna put an advert in the paper and do videos of people's wedding. What do you think?

Buddy You could do baptisms as well.

Terry Yeah – and funerals. That'd be a laugh. Close-ups on the corpse! Blimey, sounds like someone's died already.

Terry switches off the cassette player.

Carol I was listening to that.

Terry No wonder you're in such a bad mood. You need something to cheer you up. Here sing us some of your songs.

Carol I don't need cheering up. And I don't want loud music while I work. God knows why you bought him that thing. It's only going to take his mind off his school work.

Terry Oh don't start that again.

Carol Look, let's get this straight. Buddy's a clever boy and I want him to work hard for his exams. Then I want him to go to university. That way he can have a proper job and a proper future.

Terry What – stuck in some poky office when he could make records and be a star?

Carol That's just a dream.

Terry And what's wrong with dreams?

Carol They're not real. Thousands of people want to become stars – and how many make it?

Terry Some do – and Buddy'll be one of them because I'm gonna be there to make sure he is.

Buddy Hold on a minute. You're talking about me as if I'm not here. I want Buddy to do this. I want Buddy to do that. What about what I want? If you two want to argue, that's up to you. Just don't use me as an excuse. And you can stop treating me like a kid – because I'm not your kid anymore. You're the kids round here.

Buddy goes off to the band area and picks up his guitar.

Carol Now look what you've done.

Terry What I've done? You're the one who started it by being such a miserable cow. Hardly put a foot in my house and you're in a mood.

Carol It's OUR house.

Terry It's my name on the rent book.

Carol And it's my money that pays the rent.

As Terry and Carol storm off the band starts playing as Buddy sings:

SONG: ***I'm a Man and not a Boy***

You say the word and I obey
Until I feel like I will overload
You make the rules, you make the rules
But soon I will be on my own
So now I'm going down my road
You'd better think about it now I'm free
From this moment I'm listening just to me.

Chorus

Every day you treat me like a kid

I'm not your little boy, I'm not your little toy
Every day you treat me like a kid
I'm not your little boy, I'm not your little toy
'Cos I'm a man and not a boy
I'm a man and not a boy
I'm a man and not a boy, now.

I used to listen to your words
I thought you knew the best through thick and thin
But you failed, you have failed
Just look at the mess you're in
But now I've made up my own mind
I've started thinking for myself
What you taught me is going back, back on the shelf.

Chorus (Every day, etc.)

*Some fans have wandered on to watch the band
during the course of the song. The crowd grows and
applauds enthusiastically at the end of the song. The
band is pleased by the reception.*

Scene Ten

*An Office. Adrian Mandell is sitting at his desk,
working. Carol comes in with a sheet of paper.*

Carol The McSheen campaign's all booked.

Adrian Already?

Carol I'm still working on confirmation from HTV and
Central about a couple of prime-time television slots
but I'm sure they'll be OK. And all the rest are signed
and sealed.

Adrian That's terrific. You must have pushed them, they
usually take forever.

Carol Well, I've got to know a few of them over the phone
and –

Adrian Ah, that explains it – you've charmed your way into their hearts and they keep the best slots waiting for you.

Carol Not exactly.

Adrian Carol, I've got a favour to ask of you. There's some kind of panic in Milan and I ought to go across and sort it out next week. Can I leave the McSheen presentation to you?

Carol On my own?

Adrian On your own. The whole caboodle.

Carol Adrian, I can't –

Adrian Oh yes you can. You know as much about the campaign as I do. More. And you'll have old Elphick eating out of your hand – you're always the one he asks for on the phone nowadays. I'm getting quite jealous.

Carol Oh God, Adrian – a whole presentation!

Just as Carol is showing her delight, Terry comes into the office. He's filthy and dressed in his work clothes for the breaker's yard.

Terry! Oh my God, is that the time?

Terry I've been sitting in the bloody van for three quarters of an hour.

Carol I'm sorry – I got caught up with . . . with work. Adrian, this is Terry – my husband.

Adrian How do you do?

Carol Terry was giving me a lift home.

Adrian I must apologise – it's entirely my fault. I had no idea and I saddled Carol with an awful lot to do this afternoon.

Terry Is that right?

Adrian It's the price of having a talented wife.

Terry Good is she?

Adrian She's made herself indispensable. And what sort of work do you do, Mr Clark?

Terry I break things. Cars usually. Get your coat.

Carol   Terry, I –

Terry   Get your coat.

Carol cannot risk a scene so she obeys. They leave the office. Adrian watches them go into the street. Carol comes out of the office, followed by Terry.

I don't believe this. I'm the one who had to bloody wait. I'm the one you just bloody forgot about.

Carol   And I said I was sorry, didn't I? Anyway, nothing, nothing, gives you the right to treat me like that in front of my boss.

Terry   Your boss. Smarmy git. 'What sort of work do you do, Mr Clark?'

Carol   He was being polite.

Terry   Oh yeah, so polite. Except that what he was really doing was telling me I have a stinking little job – not like him and not like you. 'It's the price of having a talented wife'. I should've knocked his teeth down his throat.

Carol   That's what you can't stand, isn't it? The idea that someone might think I was talented.

Terry   I'll tell you what I can't stand. I can't stand the way you looked at him and then looked at me as if I was nothing.

Carol   Oh, really, that's just ridiculous.

Terry   And I can't stand that snobby little stuck-up voice you've started putting on.

Carol   Oh no – you want me as common as dirt, don't you?

Terry   And I can't stand it when I look at you and I don't know who you are. That's the truth, Carol. Sometimes I don't even know who you are.

Carol   Yes, well, sometimes I don't even know myself.

Terry   What the hell's that supposed to mean?

Carol   It means I don't feel the same.

Terry   About me? Why?

Carol I don't know. I tried. I really tried to be like I used to be. But I can't. I should never have come back.

Terry I'd better go then. There's a caravan at the yard. Des said I could always use it.

Terry starts away then stops.

Carol?

No reaction from Carol. He goes. Carol stands alone as the music starts. The lights fade until there is only a spot on her as she sings:

SONG: *Secrets of the Heart*

Looking glass
Do you see what I see?
Someone's standing there
Who looks a lot like me.
I know that hair
I know those dark brown eyes
But it's not me
It's only a disguise.

Chorus

Oh the secrets of the heart
Are never really shown
And even standing side by side
We still live so alone, alone.

The light goes out on Carol as another comes up on Terry on the other side of the stage. He sings:

I loved that girl
I thought that she loved me
But I found that words
Can lie so easily.
She seemed so close
She always seemed to care
But when I needed her
I found a stranger there.

Chorus (Oh the secrets of the heart, etc.)

There are lights on both Carol and Terry as, from opposite sides of the stage, they sing:

We reach out
The heart is a mystery that's never solved
Until we know ourselves
We must turn back
Maybe we'll never know
What we must do
To help us understand

Oh the secrets of the heart
Are never really shown
And even standing side by side
We still live so alone, alone.

As the song ends, the lights go out. End of Act One

ACT TWO

Scene One

In the darkness we hear a crowd chanting
'Reflections, Reflections'. The lights come up as Buddy
and the band come back on for an encore. They are
high on the music and their success.

Buddy   OK, listen – one more song and then they're gonna
kick us all out. This is a new one and I kind of wrote
it for all you lot who've come to see us here for the
last ten Saturdays. You've been really great and we
sort of feel we've got to know you.

Glenn   Yeah!

Buddy   'Course, Glenn has got to know some of you girls
really well – randy git. Anyway nowadays you get a
lot of experts going on about all kinds of problems
young people have to face – broken families, drugs
. . . And I always think – what the hell do they know
about it? We're the experts. So this song's for you. No
matter how tough it gets, just remember 'You're
gonna make it'. A-one, two, three, four.

SONG: ***It's gonna be tough***
No use in crying
But it's so hard
See the ones you really love
Fall so far apart
They swear they love you
They smile and they bluff
Let me tell you
You're gonna make it
But it's gonna be tough
It's gonna be tough
Yeah it's gonna be –

Knives and needles

38

And greed on the street
You get promises of paradise
From everyone you meet
But don't believe them
They're playing so rough
Just remember
You're gonna make it
But it's gonna be tough
It's gonna be tough
Yeah it's gonna be –

Ain't no time to sit and cry
Live your life
It's all you got
So feel alright
It's so hard today
Need a hand to fly away
Tomorrow.

Stop feeling sorry
For yourself
You got a lifetime in front of you
Don't need no help
You just need strength
And a little bit of luck
Let me tell you
You're gonna make it
But it's gonna be tough
Let me wish you good luck.

Buddy Thank you! Good night!

Mike This is our last gig here for a bit but we've got some gigs coming up at 'Mr Bigs' next month and we hope to see you there. Goodnight – you've been great.

The crowd drifts away and the band begin to put their things together or sit and drink. Elaine comes up and stands near the band together with her silent friend. Buddy is forced to notice.

Buddy Hi.

Elaine Hello.

Buddy   Did you like the gig?

Elaine   Yeah, it was great.

Elaine hands him a letter.

Buddy   What's this?

Elaine   It's for you.

Buddy   Thanks. Hey, wait a minute –

But Elaine has run away with her friend. Buddy opens the letter but Glenn grabs it from him.

Glenn   Oh, fan mail.

Buddy   Hey, Glenn, give it back.

The others hold Buddy back while Glenn reads it.

Glenn   'Dear Buddy, I've been to all the gigs and I think you're great. If you would like to go out with me I'll be at the clocktower at 7.30 on Friday. Love Elaine.' Oh, oh – we'll have to club together to buy our little singer a packet of three.

Julius   Here, you gonna turn up?

Glenn   If you don't, just pass her on to me and I'll do her a quick favour.

Jason   Yeah, so quick she won't even notice it's happened.

Glenn   Now, now – don't get all bitter and twisted just because I'm the sex symbol of the band.

Jason   Sex symbol. I don't fancy him, do you?

Glenn hands the letter back to Buddy.

Glenn   Gonna be the first is she? Losing your little cherry?

Julius   Yeah, he's been saving himself for Miss Right.

Buddy   Shut up, Jules.

Glenn   Forget Miss Right – this one is Miss Ready and Willing.

He sings.

'You're gonna make it!'

Julius   'But it's gonna be tough.'

Glenn   Don't know about tough – he's just gotta hope it's gonna be hard!

The band go off pushing Buddy and singing.

Yes, it's gotta be hard
Yes, it's gotta be hard.

Scene Two

A Pub. Dawn, a pretty 22-year-old, is reading a paper behind the bar. Terry comes up to buy a drink.

Terry   Hello, Dawn.

Dawn   Evening, Terry. The usual?

Terry   No, give me a double scotch to warm me up. Got frozen doing a video of a wedding this afternoon. And my caravan was like an ice-box when I got back. What you having, luv?

Dawn   Nothing, thanks. Landlord's night off so I'd better stay sober. There you are – that's on the house, from me.

Terry   You're an angel. Cheers.

Dawn   You ought to get a heater for that caravan now winter's coming.

Terry   Yeah, you're right. I suppose I just never thought I'd still be living there after all this time. Looks like forever now.

Dawn   Your wife must be nuts letting go of a good-looking bloke like you.

Terry   Good-looking? She thinks I'm a clapped out old Teddy Boy.

Dawn   Clapped out. You've got ten times more life in you than half the young blokes we get in here. They all look the same, too, all dressed in jeans and trainers. I reckon that's why they have adverts written on their T-shirts, so you can tell 'em apart.

Terry   And you can tell me apart, can you?

Dawn   I reckon I should have been born back in the Fifties. I love the clothes, the music. Everything.

Terry   I'm glad you weren't – it means you're still young and pretty. Fancy you liking the Fifties, though. Fabulous days they was. Go on, have a drink with me.

Dawn   Yeah, all right then.

A cinema. Buddy and Elaine make their way to the back row of the cinema lit by the flickery light from the screen. They sit.

Elaine   My friend Maureen bet me you wouldn't turn up.

Buddy   Yeah? Well she owes you some money then, doesn't she.

Elaine   She said you'd got lots of girls – like that drummer, Glenn.

Buddy   Yeah, well, I'm not like Glenn.

Elaine   Two of my friends have been out with him.

Buddy   Yeah?

Elaine   They said he was only after one thing. Sex mad.

Buddy has been trying to get his arm into a position where he could slip it round Elaine's shoulder but now takes it away.

Buddy   Well, I'm not like him.

Elaine   Oh yeah – I bet you've been out with lots of girls. The singers in the bands always get hundreds of girls.

Buddy   Not this singer.

Elaine   Oh yeah, I bet.

Buddy   It's the truth.

Elaine   How many then?

Buddy   None.

Elaine   What, since you've been a singer?

Buddy   Since ever.

Elaine   What, not ever?

Buddy   You're the first.

Elaine   Oh yeah, I bet.

Buddy It's true. I'm not the only one. Half the blokes in my class haven't been out with a girl. Everybody talks about it but . . . it's not that easy, is it?

Elaine A virgin!

Elaine puts her arms round Buddy's neck and practically devours him with a kiss. Her hands begin to creep up his thigh. Buddy emerges gasping and looks down at the advancing hand.

Buddy Bloody hell.

Before he can say anything else, Elaine's mouth clamps down on his again. The lights go out.

A Restaurant. Carol and Adrian are sitting at a table while a Waitress takes the order.

Adrian We'll start with Saumon en Papillotte and then have Roulade de Lapin Farci.

Waitress Thank you. Is the St Amour all right?

Adrian Yes, it's delicious – perfect temperature.

As the Waitress goes, Adrian raises his glass and Carol follows suit.

To you. Restaurants usually serve this too warm but when it's slightly chilled like this, I think it's my favourite wine.

Carol It's lovely.

Adrian And talking of favourite things. You said the other day that you wanted some good books to read. So I've bought you a couple of my all-time favourites. *The Prophet.* You'll love that – it's kind of philosophy about . . . well, everything. It's beautiful. And this – *The Mayor of Casterbridge.* My favourite novel.

Carol Oh Adrian, you shouldn't have –

Adrian Sorry they're not wrapped.

Carol No, it's lovely just to have them. Thanks. Oh God, there's so many things I don't know anything about – books, wine –

Adrian Ah, but the great thing is you want to learn. Most

people don't, you know. My ex-wife, for example –
she was what one would call well-educated; good
school and all that – and yet she had absolutely no
curiosity about anything.

Carol I wish I'd been well-educated. I was so useless at
school. Then when I left all I wanted to do was get
married. Now I just feel there's so much to catch up
on.

Adrian Yes, but it's precisely because you want to catch up
that you're so alive.

Carol So stupid, you mean.

Adrian Don't under-estimate yourself. You're not stupid and
you know it. Besides, I wouldn't fall in love with
someone who was stupid.

Adrian takes her hand and kisses it. The lights go out.

*The Streets of the Town. The band begins to play the
music introduction to 'Feel so Alive' as the lights come
up on Buddy and Elaine who are kissing. They break
and begin to stroll the night streets together. Buddy
sings:*

SONG: *Feel so Alive*

Never guessed that it could happen
Came like a bolt out of the blue
I was alone and so lonely
Turned around and saw you
Music loud and your eyes smiling
Seemed to tell me what to do
It was so easy and so natural
I knew I'd leave there with you.

Chorus

Took you to wake me
Took you to make me
You make me feel
You make me feel so alive
Took you to shake me
Took you to take me
You make me feel

You make me feel so alive.
You make me feel
You make me feel so alive.

*On another level we see Adrian and Carol walking.
They sing:*

We lost track of all the hours
Drinking wine in that café
And there was so much to laugh at
Cos we had so much to say.

*In another part of the space, Terry and Dawn are
strolling. Terry sings:*

Walking slowly through the city
Sheltering from that shower of rain
The moon and the stars on the river
All seemed to dance into my brain.

All six of them sing the last chorus (Took you to wake
me, etc.). *At the end of the song Buddy and Elaine
are left alone at her doorstep. They are achingly high
on the thrill of it all as they kiss.*

Elaine   I'd better go in.

Buddy   No, don't.

Elaine   I've got to.

Buddy   Can I see you tomorrow?

Elaine   Yeah, OK.

Buddy   'Night.

Elaine   'Night.

*A final kiss and Elaine goes in. Buddy walks away. He
stops and looks back at her house. He feels
wonderful. He sings a final chorus then runs off into
the night with a long shout of joy.*

Scene Three

*A Caravan. Buddy Holly is playing 'Oh Boy' on a
cassette player. Terry is singing along with it. Dawn,*

wearing not much more than one of Terry's T-shirts, is buttering some toast, standing at the table. Terry comes up behind her and gives her a cuddle and sings the last bit of the song in her ear.

Dawn Terry, get off. Are you always like this, first thing?

Terry What – randy or happy?

Dawn Both.

Terry Well, I'm always randy.

Dawn Terry – stop it!

Terry And when I'm randy I'm happy. What's the point in being miserable? I mean you're a long time dead, aren't you? Anyway you make me happy and randy.

Dawn Yeah, I also make you toast – there you are.

Terry Ta. Want some?

Terry puts a slice of toast in his mouth and offers it to Dawn. At this moment Buddy comes into the caravan.

Buddy – wotcher. Buddy – this is Dawn. Dawn – this is my boy, Buddy.

Dawn Hello.

Terry Dawn was just making some breakfast. Do you want some?

Buddy No.

Terry What's up with you?

Buddy Nothing.

Terry Anyway, cheer up, I've got some good news. I've fixed up for you to play with that Ted band I told you about. They need a new singer and they're gonna give you a try out. Great, eh? This could be the start. You and me together.

Dawn Come on, son, have some toast – there's plenty.

Buddy heads for the door.

Terry Buddy.

Buddy Tell her . . . tell her, I'm not her son.

Buddy runs out. Terry goes after him.

Terry   Buddy! Buddy, don't be like that. She didn't mean anything. Come on, don't be upset.

Buddy   Why should I be upset? After all, Mum's got Adrian Mandell, hasn't she? Oh, you don't like that, do you? Yes, she's knocking good old Adrian off every night.

Terry   Shut your mouth.

Buddy   And now you've gone and picked up this tart.

Terry slaps Buddy and Buddy goes for him. Terry traps him in his arms so that he can't actually hit out.

Terry   Buddy, stop it. Stop it. You're acting like a baby. How old are you?

Buddy   How old are you? Too old. Too damned old for her.

Terry   What do you expect me to do – stop living? Try and see it from my point of view.

Buddy   Just what Mum says. Your point of view. What about mine? You're the ones who got married, you're the ones who had me. And then when it suits you, you split up. You two just tear me in half.

Buddy starts to walk away then turns.

Oh, and another thing. You can forget that Ted band of yours 'cos I've got my own band. My own band. You don't need me. And I don't need you.

Scene Four

The Clarks' house. Carol opens the door to Adrian who's carrying a bottle of champagne.

Carol   Adrian.

Adrian   Sorry to drop in on you like this.

Carol   No, no – come in. It's lovely to see you.

Adrian   I had a couple of pieces of good news and I thought I'd come round and celebrate with you.

Carol I'm afraid it's a bit of a mess. I'm in the middle of some work I brought home actually.

Adrian You're becoming a workaholic, you know. We'll need some glasses.

Carol I'll get some.

Adrian Why don't you ask Buddy?

Carol Adrian – you know what he's like.

Adrian You never know – a bit of champagne might help to break the ice.

Carol OK.

Carol shouts out to Buddy.

Buddy, can you come down here a minute?

Carol goes off for the glasses. Buddy comes in.

Buddy What d'you want? Mum?

Adrian Hello, Buddy.

Buddy Hello. Where's my mother?

Adrian She's getting some glasses. We thought you might like to have some champagne with us.

Buddy I don't think so.

Adrian Come on, please do. We hardly ever get a chance to chat. How's your music going?

Buddy It's alright.

Adrian And school?

Buddy It's alright.

Carol enters with the glasses. Adrian starts to open the bottle.

Adrian I suppose you get a lot of prep.

Buddy What?

Adrian Prep. Homework.

Carol He's usually too busy playing his guitar.

Buddy I always do my homework. You're never here to see me do it, that's all.

The cork pops.

Adrian Right, glasses.

Carol What are we celebrating, anyway?

Adrian I've just renewed the McSheen contract – largely, and I quote Mr Elphick – because of the work you've done on the account.

Carol He said that – really?

Adrian Really. Your mother is a super businesswoman. Do you realise that? Well done, Carol. And now the other bit of news. I've been offered the Directorship of the Agency in Rome.

Carol Rome?

Buddy You're going to work in Rome?

Adrian They made me an offer I just can't refuse.

Buddy Nice one. Well, that's the sort of offer you can't refuse can you? I mean Rome – great.

Adrian The thing is, I've asked if I can take my own PA and they've agreed.

Carol Me?

Adrian It's an absolutely wonderful opportunity and it'll do your career no end of good to have that kind of experience.

Carol Well yes but . . . Rome. I mean there's Buddy's school for a start.

Adrian There's an international school in Rome. He could follow the same course as here and learn some languages first hand. It's exactly the kind of broad education one needs nowadays.

Carol Rome. Even the name sounds wonderful. What do you think, Buddy?

Buddy It doesn't matter what I think. You'll end up doing what you want, anyway. You always do.

Buddy goes.

Scene Five

*Mr Big's Club. A flashing light shows us we're at Mr
Big's where 'The Reflections' are playing a gig. The
band plays the last part of 'It's gonna be Tough'.
During this we see Terry and Dawn and Carol and
Adrian. They notice and acknowledge each other.*

SONG: ***It's gonna be Tough***

Stop feeling sorry for yourself
You've got a lifetime in front of you
Don't need no help
You just need strength
And a little bit of luck.
Let me tell you
You're gonna make it
But it's gonna be tough
It's gonna be tough
Yeah it's gonna be –
Let me wish you good luck.

Buddy   Thanks. We'd like to finish with a new one I've just
written. I'd like to dedicate it to two people who I
invited to see the band for the first time tonight – my
mum and dad. This is for you.

SONG: ***Torn in Half***

You're telling me your story
And you're handing me a line
You're giving me your point of view
But you never think of mine
You tell me that you love me
And you say I ought to laugh
Why is it that you just can't see
That I am torn in half.
Oh, I know nothing lasts
But I'm still torn in half.

The whole world is divided
Seems set to break apart
And now what you've decided

Is going to break my heart
And I will try to laugh
But I'm still torn in half.

You say that I'll get used to it
Say that nothing ever lasts
Yes, that it is your excuse for it
But I am torn in half
I know nothing lasts
But I am torn in half.

Buddy Thanks. Goodnight.

The Band go off. The crowd leaves. The two couples meet up.

Terry Hello Carol. Adrian. This is Dawn.

Carol Well, he certainly knows how to twist the knife, doesn't he?

Terry What d'you mean?

Carol Did he tell you he'd asked us?

Terry No.

Carol No, he just set it up to make us all feel awkward. And then he goes and dedicates that damn song to us.

Terry It's a great song.

Carol He says we're tearing him apart, Terry.

Terry Nah, don't take it so personal. It's a love song. I thought he was fabulous. You coming backstage.

Carol No thanks. I've had enough insults already. We're going.

Terry Suit yourself.

Carol and Adrian go. Terry addresses Dawn.

Here, go and buy yourself a drink in the bar. I want to see this lot on my own.

Dawn Terry, I don't want –

Terry Be a good girl, Dawn.

Terry goes off to the club dressing-room leaving an angry Dawn. The band is changing after the gig. They are fooling around in high spirits.

Glenn Who's got my towel? Come on – I left it there.

Mike Who's got the sex symbol's towel?

Jason Probably been nicked by one of your groupies.

Terry comes in and goes straight up to the astonished Glenn.

Terry What a drummer! What a band! And you, Buddy – I never heard you sing so good.

Buddy My dad.

Terry Terry's the name. And I'm telling you straight, I ain't seen nothing like you lot since I saw Buddy Holly in '58. A group like you could go all the way to the top. But . . . you're gonna need someone to get you there. A manager.

Buddy Hold on – we manage ourselves.

Terry You're not gonna get anywhere like that. You need someone with contacts. Someone to get you proper gigs and a record contract. You want success, right?

Mike 'Course we do.

Terry Well, you don't want it half as bad as I do. You want it – I need it. And that's why you need me – because I'll work for you like no one else will.

Buddy Look, Dad –

Terry I'll tell you what. If I haven't got you a record contract in six months you can dump me. What you say?

Jason What we got to loose?

Mike I'm in.

Julius Me, too. Glenn?

Glenn How much you gonna charge us for this?

Terry Nothing – until I get you a record contract. After that – ten per cent.

Glenn Sounds fair enough. Buddy?

Terry You and me together. Like we always dreamed of. Just give me a chance, Buddy – for six months.

Buddy OK.

Terry   Great! First off, we're gonna get some demos done. There's a little recording studio I know.

Scene Six

Small recording studio. The band are tuning up. Elaine is sitting in a corner. Des King walks in.

Des   Hello boys. Buddy.

Buddy   What you doing here?

Des   I own the place.

Buddy   Oh I get it.

Des   Yeah, a friend of mine got into a spot of bother and had to leave the country so I bought it off him cheap. Not exactly a going concern but still . . . Diversification's the name of the game. Your dad here?

Buddy   Up in the control box.

Buddy speaks into the microphone.

Dad – guess who.

Terry   Des! Come on up. It's gonna get too loud down there.

Des heads up to where Terry and Dawn are sitting in the box.

Buddy   Nice one, Dad. Do you do anything Des King's not involved in?

Terry   Shut up moaning and play the next song so we can decide how to lay it down.

Buddy   'Lay it down' – ooh, dead technical. OK, lads, ready to 'lay it down'? OK Dad, we're going to lay it down. A-one, two, three:

SONG: ***Brain Train***

Someone's looking through my eyes
My mouth is talking, telling lies
My head is filled with perfect strangers

Like a country filled with spies
One voice says 'Why not be happy?'
Another voice says 'Why not be sad?'
Both these voices are inside of me
Until I feel I'm going mad.

Chorus

Who's the driver on the brain train
Who can hear and feel and see?
Who's the driver on the brain train
'Cos I'm sure it isn't me.
Sure that it isn't me.

Where's the guard? Where's the station?
Stop this train! I scream and shout
But I'm stuck inside this carriage
Gotta ride this journey out
Gotta ride with this computer
Going crazy in my mind
Will I learn to press the right key
Before I crash right off this line.

Chorus (Who's the driver, etc.)

*Halfway through this second chorus Terry, followed
by Dawn, comes onto the floor and signals them to
stop.*

Terry　What's that supposed to be?

Julius　What's the matter with it?

Terry　It's doom and gloom that's what's the matter with it.
Nobody's gonna buy a song about some bloke going
nuts.

Buddy　It's not about going nuts. It's about how the mind
works.

Terry　Oh yeah, brilliant.

Buddy　Just 'cos it goes over your head.

Terry　There's enough misery in the world without you
singing about it. People want songs about love and
having a good time. Look, why don't you do some
oldies?

Jason   Do us a favour, Terry.

Mike   We don't want to sing crap like that.

Terry   It's not crap. You're always saying you want songs that mean things to people – well those songs meant everything to us lot in the '50s. You don't know what this dump was like when we was growing up: grey, gloomy. Then, along comes rock 'n' roll and it's like – sunshine. Another world.

Jason   Things have changed. It's not the '50s anymore, mate.

Terry   People don't change – they still want the same thing. Why do you think so many old songs are still hits today?

Buddy   I knew it would be like this. Look, the manager organises things and that's all. He does not choose the music.

Terry   I've got to like it to sell it.

Julius   Listen, you want love songs – we've got love songs. There's that new one you wrote for Elaine. Buddy?

The band go briefly into a huddle and then emerge grinning to do a 'Doo-Wop' version of:

SONG: ***Ordinary Girl***

At the end of the day
When I know I'm going to meet you
My heart just can't wait
So it races as fast as my feet do
And the very moment I take your hand
And the moment we touch
I want to tell you how much I care
But I almost can't speak 'cos I love you too much.

Chorus

Ordinary girl
It's an ordinary world we live in
But you make it special every day
Ordinary girl
It's something precious that you're giving
This ordinary guy is proud to say

I'm in love, I'm in love, I'm in love
With an ordinary girl.

Nothing has changed
Just familiar things all around me
But nothing's the same
I see with new eyes since you found me
Even the way that the wind blows cold
When we're walking at night
Just have to hold you close
You make everything good, you make everything
right.

Chorus (Ordinary girl it's an ordinary world, etc.)

Terry   That's more like it. Brilliant.

Buddy   You don't even know when you're being put on, do you?

Terry   You can take the mickey all you like. Just do stuff like that on the tour and you'll go down a bomb.

Mike   What tour?

Terry   I've fixed a tour during the Easter holidays. Give them the sheets, Dawn. Fourteen gigs in fourteen days. Newcastle, Manchester, Cardiff. Only small clubs of course, but you'll get known right across the country.

Glenn   Hold on – what Easter holidays? We're not all at school, Terry.

Terry   Well, you and Jason'll have to get time off work. Take your annual holidays then.

Glenn   My holiday's in August – I always have them then.

Terry   You're gonna have to choose, ain't you? The milk round or the band. You want me to get you to the top, you have to do what I say.

Buddy   What's this? Dawn's on the list.

Terry   Yeah. She's gonna be my assistant.

Buddy   Right, I'll bring Elaine then.

Glenn   Yeah and I'll bring some groupies.

Terry   Look, this is a professional tour. You can't just bring along some bit of stuff you just picked up.

Buddy	Why not? You are.
Terry	It's not just organising gigs, you know. I want Dawn there to fix up interviews with local papers and radio stations.
Buddy	Elaine could do that.
Terry	She's just a school kid.
Buddy	Let's have a vote. Who wants Dawn?
	No one raises their hand.
	Who wants Elaine?
	All raise their hands reluctantly.
Dawn	It's all right, Terry – I know when I'm not wanted.
Terry	Dawn!
	Terry speaks to Buddy.
	You little stirrer.
Buddy	Democratic vote.
Terry	Dawn!
	Terry goes off after Dawn who's stomped off.
Elaine	Buddy, I don't know if I can come on the tour. I'll have to ask my mum first.
Buddy	Don't be stupid – I didn't mean you were really coming.
Jason	Well, what we going to do? We can't go on without Terry.
Julius	You'll have to sort it out.
Buddy	Why me? Yeah, OK.
Mike	We may as well go off for a drink. Coming?
	Mike, Jason and Julius go off.
Elaine	Shall I come with you?
Buddy	No.
	Buddy goes off in the direction Terry went.
Glenn	That's nice, isn't it. One minute he's singing about being proud to be in love with you and the next minute he doesn't want to know. Still, you can't trust

these singers – they're always like that. Not like us drummers – quiet, faithful.

Elaine That's not what I've heard.

Glenn Yeah?

Elaine Yeah.

Glenn Well, you don't want to believe everything you hear, do you? How about coming for a drink? Cheer you up.

Elaine Yeah, all right.

Scene Seven

The Clarks' house. Buddy is packing his bag for the tour. Carol comes in. He continues packing.

Carol Buddy. Look we've got to talk about this Rome thing before you go off on tour. Buddy, please. God, you're like your father – never talk things out.

Buddy You want me to talk? OK. You want us to go off with that Mandell creep. And you want me to say 'yes' so you can feel OK about it.

Carol That's not fair. I want to do the best for both of us.

Buddy What about Dad?

Carol Look, I've been with your dad since I was seventeen and I'm caught up with him whether I like it or not. But we can't live together, even you must be able to see that. I love you. But how long before you go off living your own life? Then there's Adrian. He doesn't mean as much to me as you two, but he's been good to me and he wants me. If I go with him, I lose you and your dad. If I stay here, I end up alone. Torn in half? You don't know what it means.

Carol starts to go.

Buddy If you go to Rome – I'm staying here. I'll move in with Dad or something.

Carol   You can't do that.

Buddy   I can do what I want. I'm sixteen – I can live on my own if I want. I've been your baby and your little boy but that's all over. I've got my own life – my music, my friends. You've got to understand, Mum. This is me. It's really me.

Buddy takes his bag and goes. He joins the band who have begun playing 'This is Me'. This song becomes the centre-piece of the action that represents the tour.

SONG: ***This is Me***

Been a boy scout and a choir boy
Been a number and a name
A government statistic
A player in the game
Been a piggy in the middle
A face out in the crowd
All of that was someone else
I'm saying it out loud.

Been a bouncing little baby
The apple of their eye
Been a hero and a villain
I've been proud and I've been shy
Been the dunce out in the corner
I've been the teacher's pet
But if you think you know me
You ain't seen nothing yet.

Chorus

For the first time not the last time
This is me, it's really me
Talking off the mask right now
Stepping up to take a bow
Can you hear me, sending signals
This is me, it's really me
Making waves and making vows
Stepping up to take a bow.

I've been a heap of trouble
Been a bundle of joy

I've done good and I've done bad things
Been a happy, been a sad boy
But don't lay an image on me
I've known love and I've known hate
I've been going round in circles
Now it's time to get things straight.

Chorus (For the first time, etc.)

I've been organised and supervised and analysed and patronised
Criticised and pressurised and hypnotised and compromised.

Chorus (For the first time, etc.)

The tour ends with the end of the song.

Scene Eight

The Pub. Dawn is behind the bar as Terry comes in.

Terry I'm back.

Dawn So I see.

Terry What a tour. I'll have a scotch. Make it a double. God, it makes you feel your age knocking around with young kids. We even had to kip in the van a couple of nights. Still, it was worth it. Honestly that band is bloody great. All the club owners want 'em back. And the crowds loved 'em. I tell you, they're stars. What you having?

Dawn Nothing.

Terry And I've got some fabulous plans. For a start I've sent demo tapes off to all the record companies. And I'm gonna do a video of them down the breakers' yard. In fact, I'm gonna need your help for that.

Dawn Is that right?

Terry Yeah, I wondered if you could –

Dawn No.

Terry What?

Dawn No. 'Hello Dawn – I want you to do something'. You don't want a girlfriend you want a secretary to help run that bloody group. No, Terry, I'm not interested and I don't want to see you anymore. So why don't you rock 'n' roll off.

Elaine's house. Buddy comes to the front door and rings the bell. Elaine opens up, dressed in a dressing gown.

Elaine Buddy.

Buddy Hi. Sorry I didn't come straight round after the tour but I had a load of school work to catch up. I missed you.

Buddy kisses her but Elaine is reticent.

Buddy Your parents in?

Elaine No.

Buddy Great. We got two weeks to catch up on.

Elaine Buddy, we can't.

Buddy kisses her again.

Buddy Come on.

Elaine Listen, you gotta go.

Buddy Why?

At this moment Glenn appears behind her, dressed only in his underwear.

Glenn Come on, baby, what's keeping you? Ooops.

Buddy What's he doing here?

Elaine can only shrug.

What about us?

Elaine Well, it was nothing serious, was it?

Buddy Nothing serious? I love you. You must've known that – I told you enough times.

Glenn Look, man – I didn't realise it was like that. I thought it was just a bit of . . . Look, you can have her back if you want.

Buddy   I don't want her back now, do I?

Elaine   You pigs! What do you think I am? Get out of here. Pigs.

She pushes them both out and slams the door.

Glenn   Jesus, all my clothes are in there.

Buddy   Serves you right, you bastard. Hope you freeze to death.

Buddy goes off, leaving Glenn. A passer-by stares at him.

Glenn   Come on, Elaine. Come on, babe – open up. I didn't mean it. Be reasonable. Elaine! Elaine!

The Clarks' house. Buddy is strumming the guitar and humming the chorus of 'Love's Nothing Serious'. Carol comes in from work.

Buddy   You're late.

Carol   Have you eaten?

Buddy   Not hungry.

Carol   This place is a wreck. It wouldn't hurt you to help me by clearing up once in a while.

Buddy   What's up with you? Mum?

Carol   I've just told Adrian. I'm not going to Rome.

Buddy   Because of me?

Carol   Because of everything. What was so terrible, he was so nice about it – said he understood. Even said he'd try and get me promoted over here. That really cut me up.

Buddy   I know how you feel.

Carol   I don't think so.

Buddy   Oh yeah? Elaine's just chucked me. For a drummer.

Carol   Oh Buddy, I'm sorry.

Buddy   Thanks. I'm sorry about you and Adrian too.

Carol   I don't know what was worse, hurting him or hurting myself. I know it's right, though, love!

Buddy Yeah. Elaine told me it was nothing serious.

Carol Just tears your life apart, that's all.

Buddy Nothing Serious. It's a good title.

Buddy picks up his guitar.

Carol God, you're not . . . I don't believe you.

Buddy 'Love's nothing, nothing serious'. What did you say? Just tears your life apart?

Carol You're a vampire.

Buddy Just thinking positive. May as well get something good out of it.

Carol Well yes, but –

Buddy 'But, but . . .'. I love you when you're lost for words. In fact – forget old Adrian – I love you all the time.

Buddy gives Carol a kiss then heads off.

Carol Where you going?

Buddy Work on the song – we're doing a video at the weekend.

Scene Nine

The Breaker's yard. The band starts into 'Love's Nothing Serious'. Terry videos them.

SONG: ***Love's Nothing Serious***

Strange that they all meant so much less to you
Those lovely moments that we shared.
And sad to think that every time you held me close
Deep down inside you never cared.
I believed every loving word you said to me
I believed every promise in your kiss
I know now that they were lies you told me
But they are lies I'm gonna to miss.

Chorus

Love's nothing, nothing serious
Just tears your life apart.

Makes burning teardrops start
It only breaks your heart.
Love's nothing serious.

Friends say that one day I'll get over you
They're not the ones who feel the pain
Cos I'm the one who walks the streets at night
And hope to meet you in the rain
Well I pray that one day you'll come back to me
And that your last goodbye was not for real
That one day you are gonna change your mind
And end all this misery I feel

Chorus (Love's nothing serious, etc.)

It hurts when I hear records that we played
Think of the good times we had
At night I lie awake and think of you
The pain inside could drive me mad
Try hard to hate you for the things you've done
Those kind of feelings never last
My future's empty for the present now
My heart is still living in the past.

Chorus (Love's nothing serious, etc.)

Terry   OK, let's go again.

Jason   Give us a break – we've done it six times already.

Terry   Six? You might have to do it another sixty before I get
             enough shots for a proper video. So get on with it.

Glenn   Anybody got an aspirin?

Terry   What's up with you?

Julius   He caught a cold standing in the streets with no
             clothes on.

Buddy   With any luck it's gonna turn into pneumonia and
             he's gonna die.

Terry   Well, as long as you don't die before the fourteenth.

Glenn   Why's that?

Terry   Didn't I tell you?

Mike   Tell us what? Don't just stand there grinning – tell us
             what?

Terry   Looks as if you might have to start paying me that ten per cent we agreed on if I got you a record contract. I had a phone call from Bobby Rosen yesterday.

Jason   Who's Bobby Rosen?

Terry   The head of XS Records. I went straight up to see them. They love the demo and they want us to do a showcase for them on the fourteenth.

Scene Ten

XS Records studios. Terry and The Band are waiting in reception. Terry is smoking a big cigar. The Receptionist at the desk is on the phone. She coughs and waves the smoke away then puts the phone down.

Receptionist   Mr Rosen is on his way down.

Terry   Ta. Your new superstars.

Receptionist   Really.

Mike   God, I've got the shakes.

Terry   Relax – you'll do fine. Just let me do the talking. I know how to handle this lot.

Bobby Rosen comes in.

Bobby, you old crook. How're you doing?

Rosen   Hello, Mr Clark.

Terry   Terry – we're all professionals together, eh? Well, these are the lads – all ready to go.

Rosen   Hello. Mr Clark has –

Terry   Terry!

Rosen   Terry has probably told you we like to hear bands live before we make any decision. We pride ourselves at XS on only signing the best.

Terry   Oh yeah? I heard you were the ones who turned down Madonna. Only kidding, Bobby, only kidding.

Anyway, you'll be getting the best with this band.
Mind you, we won't be coming cheap – I know you
lot!

Buddy   Maybe we could start playing.

Rosen   Good idea. We're using Studio 2. If you'd like to go
through and set up, I'll take . . . Terry up to the
control booth.

*The lights go out. In the darkness we hear a recording
of the band playing the last part of one of their songs.
When the lights come up Terry and Rosen are in the
sound booth. Rosen talks through the mike.*

Rosen   OK, fine. If we could finish up with one more –

Terry grabs the mike.

Terry   Why don't you do an oldie – you know, an Elvis or a
Buddy Holly – just to show them what you can do.

Buddy   Come off it – we don't do oldies.

Rosen   No, we want one of yours from the demo tape. What
about 'Keep on Searching'?

Buddy   Yeah, fine.

SONG: ***Keep on Searching***

Heading for the city lights
Hoping she'll be there tonight
Looking at the girls
Are they looking at me?
Maybe down this crowded street
Suddenly our eyes will meet
I'm looking for a girl
Who's gonna love me.

Chorus

I may find her, I may not
Doesn't mean I'll ever stop
Gotta keep on searching, searching
Keep on searching, keep on
Searching for her love
I gotta keep on, keep on searching
Keep on searching, keep on

Searching for her love.

The future's such a mystery
But I believe in destiny
There's gotta be a girl
Who's thinking of me
She doesn't know that I exist
But I was born an optimist
I know that there's a girl
Who's gonna love me.

Chorus (I may find her, etc.)

Somewhere out there she is waiting
I'm gonna hold her in my arms
Somewhere out there. She is waiting
Somewhere out there.

Chorus (I may find her, etc.)

As the song ends, Rosen comes down onto the studio floor. Terry is up in the sound control booth with headphones on. Rosen talks to an engineer before addressing the band.

Rosen   Mr Clark is listening to the playback. Can you kill the mikes down here. Well, now we can talk in private. I'll be brief. You've got a lot of potential and we'd like to take an option on you. That means we'll sign you for a year and give you time to write new material. We'll give you studio time and even set up a few gigs. Meanwhile you can carry on with school or your jobs. At the end of the year if you've come up with the goods we'll sign you properly. There's one condition. We want you, but we don't want your manager. A band like you needs proper professional management and we'd be glad to point you in the right direction. The fact that we've found out that Mr Clark has a police record is not exactly a recommendation. That's our offer. I'd like your decision within twenty-four hours. Shall we go upstairs?

The lights go down. They come up with The Band standing round.

Mike   Look, we've been over it a million times – let's just vote and get it over with.

Julius   We've still got time –

Jason   Come on, we've said it all, Jules. Who wants to stick with Terry?

Buddy and Julius raise their hands.

All those who want to sign with XS.

Mike, Glenn and Jason raise their hands.

Julius   We can't do this. Terry's our mate as well as our manager.

Glenn   Democratic vote. I'll go and ring Rosen.

Jason   Who's gonna tell Terry?

They all look at Buddy.

Scene Eleven

Terry's Caravan. It is evening. Terry is inside, working at a table. Buddy comes in.

Terry   Where the hell have you been the last couple of days?

Buddy   I've been busy.

Terry   Yeah, so have I. Been designing logos for the band. And I've decided to change the name. I've drawn up a list but my favourite's 'The Bosses'. Buddy and The Bosses. What you think? Have to check it out with Bobby Rosen, of course. I tried ringing him today but he's been in meetings all the time.

Buddy   Dad.

Terry   What?

Buddy   XS want the band but . . . they don't want you as manager. Rosen found out about your prison record.

Terry   I see. Never ends, does it? Once you been in nick they never let you forget it. What do the others say?

Buddy   We had a vote. Three against two – they're gonna sign.

Terry   And you?

Buddy   We'll start again – you and me – find another band.

Terry   No.

Buddy   Dad, when you went to prison, I made a vow. I swore I'd never make you unhappy – never. And I won't.

Terry   You and me together, eh? You're a good kid, Buddy, and you couldn't make me unhappy if you tried. Listen, your mum never wanted to talk about it so we never told you but you had a brother – couple of years before we had you. Tiny little thing he was. Only saw him once. Had something the matter with his heart. He lived for five hours. Ain't fair is it? To never get a chance like him. But we're alive; we've got the chance to do things, be happy, live, not like him. That's why you're gonna sign with XS and nothing, especially me, is gonna get in your way. Right?

As Buddy nods there's a crash and a cry outside. Terry springs up and darts out followed by Buddy. Terry dashes to where two hooded men are beating up Des King. King is knocked to the ground.

Des.

The Two Men turn as Terry dashes up. Man 1 has a knife.

Man 1   Stay out of this.

He turns back to Des.

This time I'm just gonna cut you a bit, Des. Next time you don't pay, I take your eyes out.

As he bends down to cut Des, Terry charges in. Man 1 turns and sticks the knife into Terry's stomach.

Man 2   Jesus, you've done him.

Man 2 runs off. Man 1 pulls out the knife and runs off. Terry staggers and falls into Buddy's arms. Blackout. Ambulance siren. Blue flashing light.

Scene Twelve

The Hospital. Carol is pacing around. Buddy comes in carrying two plastic cups of tea.

Carol   Thanks, love. Typical, isn't it. Des King gets himself in trouble, probably for something he deserves, and it's Terry who ends up getting stabbed. You know why? Because he's known Des since they were kids. Loyalty.

Buddy   What's wrong with loyalty?

Carol   Nothing. You're wrong, you know, if you think I don't care about him. Maybe the first one you love is always . . . the one . . . whatever happens. But we can't live together, Buddy. Why does it matter so much to you?

Buddy   You know, when I was a kid the thing I loved best of all was just after I went to bed in the evening. I used to lie there and hear both of you downstairs talking, washing-up. Then sometimes Dad would put on a Buddy Holly record. It just felt so . . . safe, with both of you there.

Carol   That's the trouble with growing up – there's nowhere safe anymore.

A Doctor comes towards them.

Doctor   Mrs Clark? He's going to be all right. We had to repair a wound to the intestine but he'll be fine. Ten days and he'll be as good as new.

Carol   Can we see him?

Doctor   He's still under the anaesthetic but I'm sure Sister won't mind if you sit with him a while.

They exit. On the way, though, Buddy picks up his guitar and The Band joins in a soft version of:

SONG: ***Buddy's Song***

I always knew that sound of his
I heard it all the time

Rocking me to sleep at night
Just like a nursery rhyme
Floating warmly down the years
Sounded so alive
Singing true of love and tears
Making his voice mine.

Like seeing photos from the past
Just like a family tree
Feeling like a kid again
Belonging but still free
When days seemed twice as long and strange
With magic in the air
At night I'd lie awake in bed
And hear his voice downstairs.

Chorus

This song's for Buddy Holly
This song's for him and me
My song is for the future
His song is history.

Those childhood memories burn bright
They're all so sharp and clear
But none of them mean half as much
As that voice I used to hear
My toys and comic books have gone
I never need them now
But all those songs he used to sing
Are part of me somehow.

Chorus (This song's for Buddy Holly, etc)

Scene Thirteen

The Clarks' house. A doorbell rings. Buddy comes in and opens the door to Terry.

Buddy Dad.

Terry Wotcher, mate. Your mum in?

Buddy   Yeah, come in. Mum!

Terry   How you doing? Made any hit records yet?

Buddy   No – we're still writing new stuff. Rosen seems to like it, though.

Carol comes in.

Carol   Terry.

Terry   Hello, love. How's things?

Carol   Fine, yes.

Terry   I hear you're running the department.

Carol   Yeah.

Terry   Great.

Carol   How's the –

Terry   Oh, the scar's nearly gone now.

Carol   Do you want a coffee?

Terry   No, ta. I've got to go. Only dropped round to tell you my news, really. Just been up to Arctic Records. They were one of the companies I sent the video to, remember? Anyway they've got their own video unit and they wanted to talk to me about working for them.

Buddy   That's great.

Terry   Well, it ain't certain but it looks pretty hopeful. Even told 'em about you know what but they said they didn't give a toss about the past so . . . who knows? Well, I'd better be off.

Terry heads for the door.

Carol   Terry . . . I'm really pleased for you.

Terry   Yeah, ta.

Buddy   Hey listen – we ought to celebrate. Let's go out for a meal next week. I'll pay.

Terry   Listen to moneybags. I don't know . . . Carol?

Buddy   No strings. Honest. Just friends. You are friends, aren't you?

Carol   Yes, we're friends.

Terry The best there is.

Buddy OK – next Tuesday.

Carol We can try that new French restaurant.

Terry Oh no – I won't even understand the menu. Let's go down the pizza place.

Carol Stop putting yourself down.

Terry What me?

Carol Yes, you. I mean it.

Terry Right. See you on Tuesday.

Terry and Buddy go out onto the street.

Oh well –

Buddy I really hope the video thing works out.

Terry Don't worry about that, mate. You know me – I'm lucky. See yer.

He goes off whistling 'The One and Only' then steps in something unpleasant.

Urgh! All over me best suedes.

He shouts.

You filthy lot. Why don't you keep your dogs under control?

He laughs.

I told you I was lucky, didn't I.

He laughs again.

SONG: ***The One and Only***

I am the one and only
Nobody I'd rather be
I am the one and only
You can't take that away from me.

He goes off singing, leaving Buddy staring after him.

THE END.

QUESTIONS AND EXPLORATIONS

1 Keeping Track

Act One: Scene One

1 Why is Buddy so embarrassed in the first scene?
2 What sort of music do Buddy and Terry prefer? Do they 'get along great' as Terry says?
3 Why is the bucket so important to Julius?
4 Why does Buddy buy drinks for Terry and Carol?
5 What happens to the briefcase in this scene?

Act One: Scene Two

1 Why does Carol refuse Des's money?

Act One: Scene Three

1 Where does Buddy's interest in Buddy Holly come from?
2 What are the major differences between Carol, Buddy and Terry in this scene?
3 What was Terry like at school?

Act One: Scene Five

1 How does Buddy feel about playing in the shopping precinct?
2 What makes Buddy run off so suddenly?

Act One: Scene Six

1 What are the reasons for the confrontation between Buddy and Carol?

Act One: Scene Seven

1 What are the different characteristics of the band members?

2 Why is 'I'm Young' the most appropriate song to have in this scene?

Act One: Scene Eight

1 How believable is Terry's line 'Everything's gonna be different now'?

2 Why does Terry want to be Buddy's manager?

Act One: Scene Nine

1 How does Buddy feel about Carol and Terry's plans for his future?

Act One: Scene Ten

1 What sort of a man is Adrian Mandell?

2 'Sometimes I don't even know myself'. Why does Carol say this to Terry?

3 What are the major differences between Terry and Carol in this scene?

Act Two: Scene One

1 What is the relationship between the band members like?

Act Two: Scene Two

1 What do you think Dawn sees in Terry?

2 Why does Elaine think Buddy has been out with lots of girls?

Act Two: Scene Three

1   Why does Buddy try to hit Terry?

Act Two: Scene Four

1   What is the good news that Adrian brings to Carol?

Act Two: Scene Five

1   Why is Carol so angry?
2   What offer does Terry make to the band?

Act Two: Scene Six

1   Why is 'Brain Train' an appropriate song for this scene?
2   What do we find out about the band members in this scene?

Act Two: Scene Seven

1   What do we discover about Carol in this scene?

Act Two: Scene Eight

1   What happens to the relationships between the characters in this scene?

Act Two: Scene Nine

1   What is the good news that Terry gives to the band?

Act Two: Scene Ten

1   Why doesn't Mr Rosen want the band and Terry?
2   What decision does the band take? Do you think they were right?

Act Two: Scene Eleven

1 Why does Terry tell Buddy to go ahead without him?

Act Two: Scene Thirteen

1 What do we find out about Buddy, Carol and Terry from this scene?

2 Explorations

Characters

1 Draw silhouettes of Buddy, Carol and Terry.

On the outside of each silhouette write notes about the pressures and influences that the characters feel from other people and events in their lives. Inside each silhouette write notes about the inner hopes, fears and concerns that make the character who they are.

For each of the characters discuss how far their actions are shaped by outer events and how much by their own desires.

2 Write a school report for Buddy. You will need to use your imagination about some of the subjects as well as the evidence you have from the play.

3 What happens to Buddy after the end of the play?

a) Improvise scenes that take place a day, a week and a year later.

b) Write the scene that is the family meal planned for next Tuesday.

4 Discuss the relationships between the following men and women portrayed in the play.

Carol and Terry

Carol says: 'You're wrong, you know, if you think I don't care about him. Maybe the first one you love is always ... the one ... whatever happens. But we can't live together, Buddy.'

Why can't Carol and Terry live together? What do you think happened to them over the years?

Carol and Adrian

Why is Carol attracted to Adrian?

Do you think Carol was right not to go to Rome?

Terry and Dawn

'You don't want a girlfriend, you want a secretary ...'

Did Terry want a girlfriend? Was his relationship with Dawn ever likely to succeed?

Buddy and Elaine

How is Buddy's relationship with Elaine contrasted with the relationships between the adults in the play?

5 Imagine Buddy at Terry's age. Write a poem or a song looking back at what he has achieved and looking forward to his hopes for the future.

6 Write notes for one of the actors in the play. What would you expect them to look like? How should they play the character? What skills do they need and what emotions should they use?

From Novel to Play

1 Find a copy of Nigel Hinton's original novel of *Buddy's Song*. If you have enjoyed the play you will probably enjoy reading the novel too.

a) Make notes about the differences between the novel and the play.

b) Why do you think the play starts with a different scene?

c) Why do you think the play shows us more of the relationships between the adult characters? (In the book, we mostly learn about their relationships through their effect on Buddy.)

d) What is the function of the songs in the play?

2 Choose a particular scene from the play and find the same section in the novel.

a) What changes did Nigel Hinton make to adapt the scene for the stage?

b) Do the characters say and do things in exactly the same way as they do in the book? If not, why not?

c) What has Nigel Hinton added? What has he taken away?

d) Do you think the scene works best in novel form or in play form?

Drama

1 Find a moment in the play when a character is faced with a choice.

a) Act the moments immediately before the choice, stopping the action at the point a decision needs to be made.

b) Act the scene out again with two other members of your group playing 'devil' and 'angel' giving advice on each shoulder of the character.

c) What would happen if the character made a different decision? Improvise the scene that follows.

2 Select a favourite character from the play. Write a monologue for your character in which they reflect upon their lives. How do they reveal their thoughts?

In Performance

1 Choose any moment from a scene that includes Buddy, Carol and Terry. Work in groups of four. One person should mould the other three into a position that most effectively shows the attitude of each character and what is happening in the scene.

When everyone is 'frozen' you can touch the characters on the shoulder. They must then tell you how the character is feeling.

Repeat this exercise with other scenes and other characters in the play.

2 In groups of four, pretend to be the Clark family's neighbours. You are gossiping about the family. Select some overheard conversations that reflect the comings and goings of the different people in the play. Act your conversations before the rest of the class.

Music

1 Write profiles of three characters in the play who have different opinions about music. In groups discuss why different people like different styles of music.

2 'There's enough misery in the world without you singing about it.'

Do you agree? Find (recent) examples of songs you know Terry would consider miserable. Discuss their good points.

GLOSSARY